Dr. Michael Leach
and Dr. Meriel Lland

The World of Animals

illustrated by
Juanita Londoño-Gaviria

ARCTURUS

ARCTURUS

This edition published in 2022 by Arcturus Publishing Limited
26/27 Bickels Yard, 151–153 Bermondsey Street,
London SE1 3HA

Authors: Dr. Michael Leach and Dr. Meriel Lland
Illustrator: Juanita Londoño-Gaviria
Designer: Suzanne Cooper
Design Manager: Jessica Holliland
Editor: Donna Gregory
Proofreader: Cassie Armstrong
Editorial Manager: Joe Harris

ISBN: 978-1-3988-2023-4
CH008293NT
Supplier 42, Date 0922, PI 00001002

Printed in Singapore

CONTENTS

ANIMAL PLANET

Animals live on every continent and habitat, from the depths of the oceans to the highest mountains. There is so much to learn about and from them, so we can better understand them and learn how to protect them. Whether they are familar creatures we see in our everyday lives or shy, exotic animals that hide out of sight, all animals have a part to play in maintaining balance on the Earth. Some are vital in pollination and seed dispersal, while others are food for predators, including humans. Many are intelligent and work cooperatively in groups, while others are loners. All are fascinating.

SEVEN CONTINENTS

Most of the Earth's land lies in seven continents—Africa, Europe, North America, South America, Asia, Antarctica, and Oceania. Oceania covers Australia and New Zealand, together with the 25,000 islands of the Pacific.

HABITATS: A PLACE TO CALL HOME

A habitat is an environment in which animals and plants live—somewhere they can find food, shelter, and a safe place to raise young. The position of the continents on the Earth's surface has a huge effect on habitats. There are six major habitat types: freshwater, sea, forest, desert, grassland, and tundra. Habitats are created by weather and temperature. For example, forests can only exist where there is enough rainfall, and deserts can only form when there is very little rain.

NORTH AMERICA

SOUTH AMERICA

1: TUNDRA

2: FOREST

3: GRASSLAND

4: DESERT

5: SEA

6: FRESHWATER

ASIA

EUROPE

AFRICA

OCEANIA

ADAPTATION

Animals already lived on Pangea when it started to fragment. They slowly evolved as the land moved, adapting to the new conditions. For example, species in forests started to climb and find food in the trees. Some grew thick hair against the biting cold of the Arctic, others became nocturnal to avoid the daytime temperatures of a hot desert. Even now, most species can only survive in a small number of habitats.

HOW IT ALL BEGAN—PANGEA

The Earth has not always looked like it does today. Millions of years ago, most of the land on the planet was joined together in one massive area called Pangea. Pangea lasted for about 100 million years and eventually fragmented. Chunks of land that we call "continents" changed position, driven by powerful movements in the Earth's surface. The continents are still moving. As you read this book, Europe and North America are steadily shifting farther apart by about 2.5 cm (1 in) every year.

ANTARCTICA

WHAT IS THAT ANIMAL?

Scientists estimate that there are nearly 9 million living animal species. But new ones are discovered almost every week.

Animals are split into groups that help us study their evolution, the ways in which they behave, and the role they play in their ecosystem. The groups are worked out by asking questions. The first is "Does that species have a backbone?" Animals with a backbone are called vertebrates, such as mammals, birds, and reptiles. Species without a backbone are called invertebrates, like insects, worms, and spiders. They are then split into even smaller groups by asking more questions, such as: "Does this animal have feathers" or "Does this animal have cold blood?" Using these answers, animals can be put into a family with similar species.

WARM- OR COLD-BLOODED?

Most animals are ectothermic, or cold-blooded. Their body temperature is similar to the temperature of their environment. Mammals and birds are endothermic or warm-blooded. They generate their own heat, so they can thrive in cooler habitats.

KEY FEATURES OF SPIDERS

- Eight legs.
- Body split into two sections.
- Body is inside a hard shell called an exoskeleton.
- No wings.

KEY FEATURES OF REPTILES

- Have a backbone.
- Cold-blooded.
- Covered in scales.

KEY FEATURES OF MAMMALS

- Have a backbone.
- Give birth to live young.
- Have hair.
- Warm-blooded.
- Feed young on milk produced by mother.

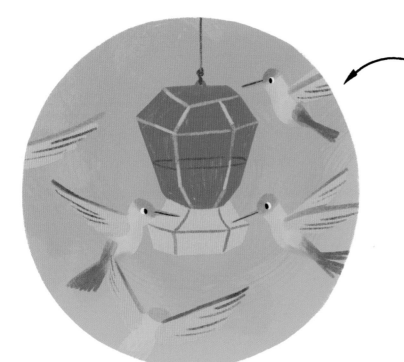

KEY FEATURES OF BIRDS

- Have a backbone.
- Covered in feathers.
- Warm-blooded.
- Lay eggs.

SCIENTIFIC NAMES

Animals have names in many languages. For example, "polar bear" is English but in Norway it is called *isbjørn* and in Finland it is *jääkarhu*. This can cause confusion. About 250 years ago, a scientist called Carl Linnaeus made things easier. He gave every species one name that could be used by everyone, whatever language they spoke. Today, animals have a local name plus a two-word scientific name. The first shows what family it belongs to and the second shows exactly what species it is. The polar bear's scientific name is *Ursus maritimus*.

KEY FEATURES OF INSECTS

- Body is divided into three parts.
- Have six legs.
- Body is inside a hard shell called an exoskeleton.

AFRICA

Africa is famous for wide, grassy plains that are alive with great herds of grazing animals and the "big five"—lion, elephant, rhino, buffalo, and leopard—but there is so much more to discover in this exciting continent. Africa is home to tropical swamps, the world's largest hot desert, and even snow-covered mountains.

The Equator crosses Kenya, Congo, and Gabon. This creates hot, rich habitats that support a wealth of wildlife, but the extreme north and south of the continent and the mountainous regions can be cold in winter.

Scientists believe that Africa was home to the very first humans around 300,000 years ago. Today, 54 countries share the diverse landscape of the continent with a huge range of animals. Thousands of penguins nest on the coast near Cape Town in South Africa, just a very short way away while lions hunt in Addo Elephant National Park, while great white sharks patrol the deep water surrounding the Cape. These legendary species attract millions of visitors every year, but there are still parts of Africa that have not been fully explored by scientists. New animal species are regularly discovered in the dense Congo rain forest, for example, and it is home to wildlife that we have yet to study fully.

1 **NILE DELTA**

The Nile River brings life to the desert lands of Egypt. Lush vegetation attracts insects into the region—sometimes in huge swarms!

2 **ATLAS MOUNTAINS**

The Atlas is an area of high mountains, deserts, and fertile valleys. The animals that live here include wolves, tiny foxes with huge ears, and painted frogs.

3 **THE SAHEL**

Arabic for "edge," the Sahel edges the Sahara desert and the forests of the south. Animals here have to be tough and able to survive frequent drought. They include sand cats and egg-eating snakes!

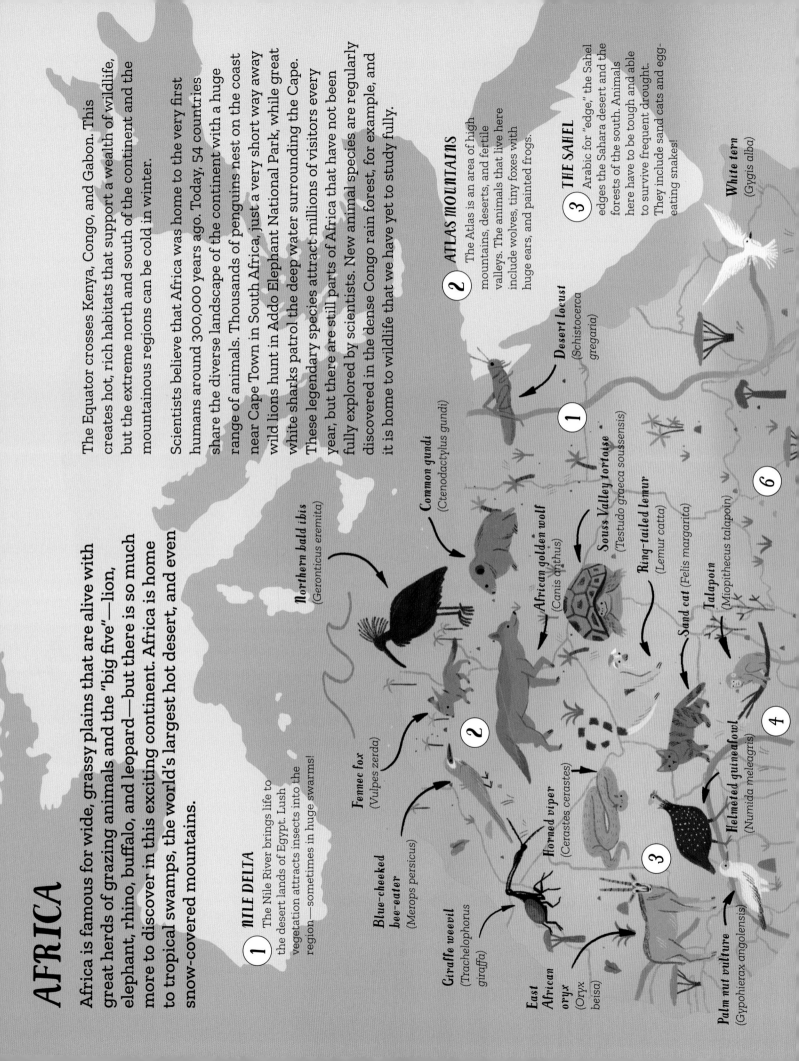

Northern bald ibis
(Geronticus eremita)

Common gundi
(Ctenodactylus gundi)

Desert locust
(Schistocerca gregaria)

Fennec fox
(Vulpes zerda)

African golden wolf
(Canis anthus)

Souss Valley tortoise
(Testudo graeca soussensis)

Ring-tailed lemur
(Lemur catta)

Sand cat (Felis margarita)

Talapoin
(Miopithecus talapoin)

Blue-cheeked bee-eater
(Merops persicus)

Horned viper
(Cerastes cerastes)

Helmeted guineafowl
(Numida meleagris)

Giraffe weevil
(Trachelophorus giraffa)

East African oryx
(Oryx beisa)

Palm nut vulture
(Gypohierax angolensis)

White tern
(Gygis alba)

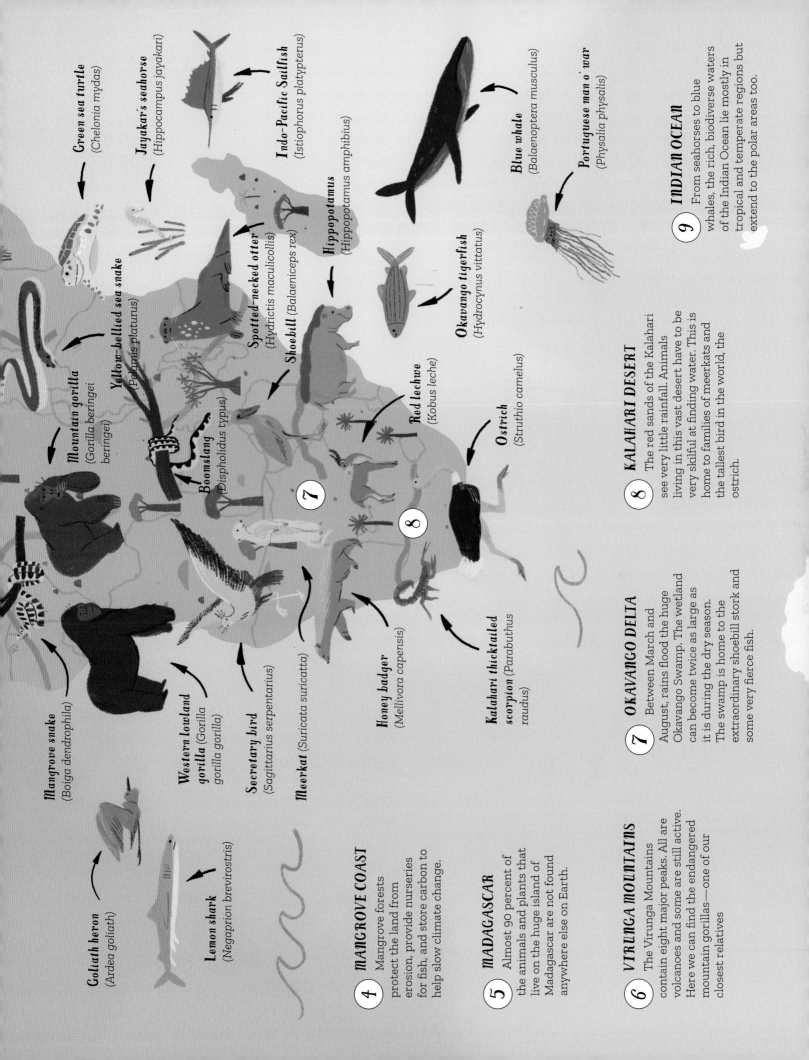

Green sea turtle
(*Chelonia mydas*)

Jayakar's seahorse
(*Hippocampus jayakari*)

Indo-Pacific Sailfish
(*Istiophorus platypterus*)

Blue whale
(*Balaenoptera musculus*)

Portuguese man o'war
(*Physalia physalis*)

Hippopotamus
(*Hippopotamus amphibius*)

Spotted-necked otter
(*Hydrictis maculicollis*)

Shoebill (*Balaeniceps rex*)

Yellow-bellied sea snake
(*Pelamis platurus*)

Mountain gorilla
(*Gorilla beringei beringei*)

Mangrove snake
(*Boiga dendrophila*)

Boomslang
(*Dispholidus typus*)

Okavango tigerfish
(*Hydrocynus vittatus*)

Red lechwe
(*Kobus leche*)

Ostrich
(*Struthio camelus*)

Western lowland gorilla (*Gorilla gorilla gorilla*)

Secretary bird
(*Sagittarius serpentarius*)

Meerkat (*Suricata suricatta*)

Honey badger
(*Mellivora capensis*)

Kalahari thicktailed scorpion (*Parabuthus raudus*)

Goliath heron
(*Ardea goliath*)

Lemon shark
(*Negaprion brevirostris*)

9 **INDIAN OCEAN**

From seahorses to blue whales, the rich, biodiverse waters of the Indian Ocean lie mostly in tropical and temperate regions but extend to the polar areas too.

8 **KALAHARI DESERT**

The red sands of the Kalahari see very little rainfall. Animals living in this vast desert have to be very skilful at finding water. This is home to families of meerkats and the tallest bird in the world, the ostrich.

7 **OKAVANGO DELTA**

Between March and August, rains flood the huge Okavango Swamp. The wetland can become twice as large as it is during the dry season. The swamp is home to the extraordinary shoebill stork and some very fierce fish.

6 **VIRUNGA MOUNTAINS**

The Virunga Mountains contain eight major peaks. All are volcanoes and some are still active. Here we can find the endangered mountain gorillas—one of our closest relatives

5 **MADAGASCAR**

Almost 90 percent of the animals and plants that live on the huge island of Madagascar are not found anywhere else on Earth.

4 **MANGROVE COAST**

Mangrove forests protect the land from erosion, provide nurseries for fish, and store carbon to help slow climate change.

LOCUSTS

Locusts (*Schistocera gregaria*) usually live solo or in small groups, eating the few plants that survive in the desert of the Nile Delta. When a drought occurs, the starving locusts do something astonishing—they grow longer wings and take flight! They join other locusts and soon there can be 150 million insects flying together. The swarms cover up to 800 sq km (300 sq mi). There are so many locusts that they block out the sunlight.

When they finally find lush crops, the ravenous insects start to eat and don't stop until the field is bare! The Nile wetland, or delta, has rich, fertile soil and is ideal for growing food plants, such as corn and rice. Here, the river slows, becomes shallow, splits into channels, and widens out. For the farmers of the Nile Delta, locust swarms pose a huge threat.

Voracious appetite

For small-scale farmers, loss of crops can lead to famine. In just one day, a swarm of 80 million locusts can eat the same amount of food as 35,000 people.

Defender ducks

Some villages threatened by swarms keep armies of domestic ducks (*Anas platyrhynchos dom*) that graze among their crops. These birds love eating locusts—around 200 each day per duck!

Swarmers and loners

Locusts are full of surprises. Eggs hatch into wingless young called "hoppers." In response to environmental conditions, hoppers develop into winged adults, which show two different ways of behaving: some are very sociable and will swarm while others stay solitary. Social locusts are more active, larger, have longer wings, and turn bright yellow.

A tasty snack

Hungry? Try a locust kebab! Grilled, baked, or skewered, people have been eating locusts as a nutritious delicacy for centuries.

Time to feast

Swarms mean a feeding bonanza for animal predators such as black-winged kites (*Elanus caeruleus*), which follow the flying feast.

NORTH AFRICA

Picture Africa and you think of sunshine and perhaps monsoon rains, but one region of the continent sees huge snowfalls! This place is the wild Atlas mountain range. This is 2,500 km (1,600 mi) long, reaches a height of 4,167 m (13,671 ft), and passes through three countries. Different areas of the range have very different environmental conditions. In winter, the high mountains are hostile, but the weather is always warmer and less windy at lower altitudes. Here, on the lower slopes, there are rich forests providing shelter for wildlife.

Blue-cheeked bee-eater
(Merops persicus)
Bee-eaters sit on high perches watching for bees or other insects. They dart out and catch prey in midair.

Barbary sheep
(Ammotragus lervia)
Very agile and hardy, these sheep can leap rocks and scramble up steep cliffs.

Moroccan painted frog
(Discoglossus scovazzi)
At the end of winter, the snow melts and creates small ponds that are ideal places for these frogs to live, feed, and lay eggs.

Temminck's lark
(Eremophila bilopha)
Every spring, males grow two small pointed feathers on the top of their head—these give the bird its local name of horned lark.

African golden wolf
(Canis anthus)
These are not often seen but their eerie voices can be heard as they howl, whine, and cackle in the high mountains.

The position of the Atlas Mountains, sandwiched between the Mediterranean Sea to the north and the Sahara Desert in the south, means that the area is largely isolated from the rest of the continent. The Atlas Mountains have become home to some extraordinary creatures found nowhere else on Earth.

Spain

Mediterranean Sea

Morocco

Atlas Mountains

Algeria

Northern bald ibis (*Geronticus eremita*)
This distinctive bird nests on high cliffs.

Barbary partridge (*Alectoris barbara*)
These are noisy birds that nest in shallow scrapes on the ground.

Souss Valley tortoise (*Testudo graeca soussensis*)
These very rare tortoises are found in a few areas of the Atlas Mountains.

Koelliker's glass lizard (*Hyalosaurus koellikeri*)
These lizards have no forelimbs and very small hind legs. They look like snakes but notice their eyes. Snake eyes are always open, even during sleep. Lizards have eyelids that close, so if it blinks, it must be a lizard.

Fennec fox (*Vulpes zerda*)
Their huge ears can swivel around to locate the tiny noises made by their prey.

Amata moth (*Amata alicia*)
Caterpillars like eating the leaves of the coffee plants grown in Morocco.

Common gundi (*Ctenodactylus gundi*)
This gundi likes to sunbathe on rocks in the early morning.

THE SAHEL

The Sahel is a vast dry or semi-arid area south of the Sahara Desert. It stretches across all of Africa from west to east. This is one of the world's hottest places and temperatures can reach nearly 50°C (122°F). Climate change means that the region is slowly getting bigger and hotter. The Sahel gets very little rain and strong winds regularly remove the top layer of soil, leaving a landscape of rocks and sand. This is called soil erosion and provides a harsh environment for plants and animals. Sometimes there is no rainfall for five months, so animals that live in the Sahel have to survive long periods without drinking and often travel great distances to find food and water.

Mediterranean Sea

Sahara Desert

Sahel

Atlantic Ocean

Sahel paradise-whydah *(Vidua orientalis)*

In the breeding season, males grow long tail feathers that are used to attract a mate.

Horned viper *(Cerastes cerastes)*

These snakes are perfectly camouflaged in the rocky desert as they hunt lizards and small mammals.

East African oryx *(Oryx beisa)*

These oryx raise their body temperature during periods of drought to avoid losing water through their sweat.

Sand cat *(Felis margarita)*

Long hairs cover the soles of their paws to protect the pads against the extreme temperatures of the desert.

Saharan silver ant *(Cataglyphis bombycina)*

The fastest ant in the world, they can run at 1 m (3.28 ft) a second, which is the average speed of a walking human.

Peter's banded skink (*Scincopus fasciatus*)

Skinks are lizards and lizards have an extraordinary trick: if they are attacked, their tail can be dropped! It wriggles violently to distract the predator while the lizard escapes.

Golden nightjar
(*Caprimulgus eximius*)

This nocturnal bird feeds at night. It sings at dawn and dusk from its roost on the ground.

Red-billed quelea
(*Quelea quelea*)

Here's a good fact: this is the most numerous wild bird in the world.

Helmeted guineafowl
(*Numida meleagris*)

Guineafowl are great at finding and eating flies, ticks, and locusts.

Egg-eating snake (*Dasypeltis sahelensis*)

These snakes hunt eggs! They have no venom to kill prey but their mouths are big enough to swallow an egg larger than their own head—whole!

Desert crocodile
(*Crocodylus suchus*)

Desert crocs regulate their body temperature by sitting in water. During drought, when water is scarce, they dig deep holes in the sand to keep cool.

Goliath heron (*Ardea goliath*)
The world's tallest heron, it reaches 1.5 m (5 ft) tall and has a 2.3 m (7.5 ft) wingspan.

Fiddler crab
(*Afruca tangeri*)
Males have one huge front claw that is used to signal to potential mates and warn off rivals.

Palm nut vulture
(*Gypohierax angolensis*)
Ever heard of a (mostly) vegetarian vulture? As their name suggests, these eat the fruit of palm trees and only occasionally feed on meat.

MANGROVES

Mangrove swamps grow in hot places where the land meets the sea. There are at least 50 species of mangrove tree and these are the only ones in the world that cope with the ebb and flow of tides and with life in salty seawater. They grow well in the thick, black mud on the coast and have evolved to survive surging storms. When the sea is at low tide, the mangroves' strange aerial roots are visible. These act like stilts to support the trees; they also absorb oxygen from the air, which the mangroves need to live.

This unique habitat provides a nursery for many species of fish and a home to shellfish. Mussels cling to the aerial roots and open and close their shells with the tide. At low tide, birds search for worms and small crabs in the mud between the roots. At high tide, fish swim and hide in the same places.

Lemon shark (*Negaprion brevirostris*)
Young sharks hunt for small fish hiding among the mangrove roots.

Blue-breasted kingfisher
(Halcyon malimbica)

These birds move to wetter habitats in the dry season.

West African Mangrove Coast

Atlantic Ocean

Talapoin
(Miopithecus talapoin)

This is Africa's smallest monkey. They always live close to water and swim very well.

African bullfrog
(Pyxicephalus adspersus)

This frog weighs up to 1.5 kg (3.3 lb). They can jump as far as 1.8 m (6 ft)—several times the length of their own body.

Blanding's tree snake
(Toxicodryas blandingii)

These are ambush predators; they don't chase their prey but wait for it to approach them. Then they strike.

Mud skipper
(Periophthalmus barbarus)

Think all fish live in water? Think again! Skippers can breathe in both water and air. Their super-strong front fins work like legs so they can walk on land and even climb trees.

MADAGASCAR

Madagascar, an island slightly larger than France, is full of surprises. About 90 percent of its wildlife live only in this one place.

The island was originally part of Asia. About 88 million years ago, it split away from India and became a giant island surrounded by seas that are home to some of the world's biggest sharks. Some African birds flew to Madagascar, but mammals and reptiles could not cross the dangerous sea. Creatures that had been carried over from Asia slowly changed and evolved into completely new species. Animals that live in one place only are called endemic species."

Indian Ocean

Madagascar

Mozambique Channel

Giraffe weevil (*Trachelophorus giraffa*)
Male giraffe weevils have extremely long necks that are used to wrestle other males.

Indri (*Indri indri*)
Indris are the world's largest lemur.

Dugong (*Dugong dugon*)
Dugongs—or "sea cows"—breathe air but spend their lives in the sea, eating plants known as seagrass.

Golden trevally (*Gnathanodon speciosus*)
Golden trevally snap up invertebrates disturbed by the dugongs as they feed.

Tomato frog (*Dyscophus antongilii*)
The bright red shade is a warning sign that it is poisonous.

Sunset moth (*Chrysiridia rhipheus*)
Unlike most moths, sunset moths fly in daylight.

Nano-chameleon (*Brookesia nana*)
This tiny species is as long as a human fingernail is wide and is probably the world's smallest reptile.

Crested coua (*Coua cristata*)
These birds are omnivores—their diet includes seeds, insects, eggs, and chameleons.

Ring-tailed lemur (*Lemur catta*)
Ring-tailed lemurs live in family groups and are closely related to monkeys and apes.

Gorillas for different climates

There are different kinds of gorillas. Western lowland gorillas (*Gorilla gorilla gorilla*) live in hot forests, have short hair, and the hair on the top of their head is reddish. Mountain gorillas (*Gorilla beringei beringei*) live in cooler forests and have darker, thicker hair.

Distinctive males

Adult male gorillas have a long, strong bone running over the top of their skull. This anchors their powerful jaw muscles and makes their heads appear almost pointed.

Family-based groups

Gorillas live in close family groups of between two and 40 individuals. As they get older, the hair on their back turns silvery grey.

Gorillas are gentle, intelligent herbivores. They eat leaves, shoots, and fruit.

Head of the family

A gorilla leader is called a silverback. The silverback is the most knowledgeable, strongest, and, usually, the oldest male. He is the protector of the group and uses his experience to decide where to lead the group to eat or sleep.

GORILLAS

Mountain gorillas (*Gorilla beringei beringei*) are one of the world's largest primates. They are muscular, with broad hands and feet and a massive chest. A fully gown male can weigh 250 kg (550 lb), which is approximately the weight of three adult humans. Gorillas behave in some human-like ways, and can laugh and show sadness.

Mountains gorillas live in the rain forests of Central Africa and the Virunga Mountains. A rain forest is a woodland that receives more than 2.54 m (100 in) of rain in a year. These wet, often warm, forests encourage high levels of biodiversity—that is, many different species of plants and animals.

Gorillas are threatened by loss of their forest home and by poaching. Rangers, local communities, and international charities protect the endangered mountain gorillas, and in recent years their numbers have risen to approximately 1,000 individuals.

Virunga Mountains

Lowland Gorillas

Mountain Gorillas

Unique marks
Gorillas have fingerprints

Showing emotion
When angry, gorillas slap the palms of their hands to their chests to make lots of alarming noise. This is called a display.

Monkeying around
Adult gorillas spend most of their time on the ground, but young gorillas enjoy playing high up in the trees.

Staying close
Mothers give birth every four to six years. Baby gorillas stay with their mothers until they are around two years old.

OKAVANGO DELTA

The Okavango Delta is an enormous oasis in a very dry country. The Okavango River starts in Angola and flows south into Botswana, where it slowly soaks into the ground. This is called an inland delta and it produces an area of precious wetland and swamp. The Okavango is the largest inland delta in the world.

This lush habitat is full of grasslands for grazing and lagoons, many of which can be explored by canoe. Part of the Okavango is permanently flooded while other areas of the wetland swell as the result of seasonal rains farther north. Hot daytime temperatures, a plentiful water supply, and fertile soil mean that plants and animals thrive here. Some animals live here year-round while others arrive as the dry season makes water scarce in other areas. This is one of the best places in Africa to watch wildlife.

Pel's fishing owl
(Scotopelia peli)

This owl fishes at night. It sits on a branch above the water and swoops down to catch fish in its talons.

Boomslang
(Dispholidus typus)

Boomslang is the Afrikaans word for tree snake. They live high up in the branches, hunting for lizards and frogs.

Shoebill *(Balaeniceps rex)*

Named after its huge beak, the shoebill is also called the whale-headed stork. They hunt fish and frogs in shallow water.

Spotted-necked otter
(Hydrictis maculicollis)

These otters have webbed feet and spend most of their lives hunting fish and frogs.

Okavango tigerfish
(Hydrocynus vittatus)

Tigerfish are powerful hunters armed with very sharp teeth. They have been seen jumping out of the water to catch birds that come down to drink.

Red lechwe (*Kobus leche*)

These antelope spend most of their lives standing in water. They have a waterproof coating on their legs to prevent damage to their skin. They sometimes gather in giant herds of up to 5,000 animals.

Hamerkop (*Scopus umbretta*)

Hamerkops are only 56 cm (22 in) high but they build one of the world's biggest nests. It has walls and a roof, contains around 8,000 twigs, and measures 1.5 m (5 ft) wide.

Giant pill millipede (*Sphaerotherum* species)

Pill millipedes get their name from their habit of curling up into a tight ball when in danger.

Hippopotamus (*Hippopotamus amphibius*)

The word hippopotamus means "water horse." They spend their days in water hiding from the strong sun and graze at night.

African jacana (*Actophilornis africanus*)

Jacana are also called lily-trotters. Their long toes and claws spread the birds' weight allowing them to "trot" on the lily leaves that float on Okavango's numerous waterways.

Angolan reed frog (*Hyperolius parallelus*)

This multihued frog makes its home on vegetation at the edge of swamps and lakes.

South Central Africa

Okavango Delta

Namibia

Botswana

Atlantic Ocean

South Africa

Indian Ocean

KALAHARI DESERT

The Kalahari region is a landscape of red sand dunes and plains dotted with spiky grasses and camelthorn trees. The Kalahari gets its name from the word *Kgala*— which means "great thirst" in the local Tswana language. Summers are very hot with little or no rainfall. At this time, most of the Kalahari's lakes dry out, leaving lakebeds of crunchy salt crystals. These are called salt pans and they cover an incredible 16,000 sq km (6,200 sq mi). The pans flood once more after the rains return and, for a time, become home to many wildlife species.

This pattern of drought and flood—dry and wet seasons— shapes the Kalahari. As the floods recede, the animals have to travel greater and greater distances to find food and water. Today, there is a new threat to Kalahari wildlife as humans overgraze cattle on land where there is already little for the wild animals to eat.

Atlantic Ocean

Kalahari Desert

Indian Ocean

Ostrich (*Struthio camelus*)

Ostrich eggs are the biggest in the world. They are 15 cm (6 in) long and weigh 1.35 kg (3 lb). Each is so strong that an adult human can stand on it without the shell breaking.

Desert rain frog (*Breviceps macrops*)

Unlike most frogs, this species has no tadpole stage. They emerge from their eggs as fully-formed tiny frogs.

Thick-tailed scorpion (*Parabuthus raudus*)

The venom of these scorpions has been known to be fatal for humans.

Shovel-snouted lizard (*Meroles anchietae*)

In very high temperatures, these lizards lift their legs in turn to stop their feet from burning on the hot sand.

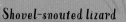

Pygmy falcon (*Polihierax semitorquatus*)
This is Africa's smallest bird of prey and weighs approximately the same as eight average-sized grapes!

Meerkat
(*Suricata suricatta*)
Meerkats live in groups of up to 30 and always have a sentinel on duty to watch for danger. They eat insects, lizards, and birds' eggs.

Caper white butterfly
(*Belenois aurota*)
Populations of these butterflies gather in huge clouds that can be blown long distances by the strong winds.

Honey badger (*Mellivora capensis*)
Honey badgers are highly intelligent, excellent at escaping captivity, and have even been known to drive off lions.

Secretary bird
(*Sagittarius serpentarius*)
These birds kill their prey by the sharp stamping of their powerful feet.

Six-eyed sand spider (*Sicarius hahni*)
These very flat spiders hunt by hiding in the sand until they feel the vibrations of an insect walking nearby—then they pounce!

INDIAN OCEAN

The Indian Ocean is huge. It is over five times larger than the USA and covers almost one fifth of the world's surface. It is the warmest of all the oceans and stretches from north of the Equator down to the Antarctic. Water temperatures range dramatically from 30°C (86°F) to freezing point. It contains a huge variety of animal species, including endangered turtles, seals, and dugongs.

Few marine creatures live in the deepest parts of the Indian Ocean, the Java Trench, where it is dark and very cold. Only highly specialized animals can tolerate the water pressure near the seabed. Most species are found closer to the surface and in shallower water, where it is warmer and there is plenty of food. Animals living in any ocean don't have a fixed territory—they are constantly on the move in response to changes in wind direction, temperature, and sea currents.

Yellow-bellied sea snake (*Pelamis platurus*)
Sea snakes eat, sleep, and give birth in the water.

Mauritian flying fox (*Pteropus niger*)
These animals are large fruit bats with a wingspan of 80 cm (31 in) and a fox-like face. They help pollinate many species of plant on Mauritius.

White tern (*Gygis alba*)
White terns do not build nests. They lay one egg and balance it between the branches of a tree.

Blue whale (*Balaenoptera musculus*)
The blue whale is the largest animal that has ever lived on Earth. At 30 m (100 ft) long and weighing more than 180,000 kg (200 tons), it is bigger than any dinosaur.

Jayakar's seahorse
(Hippocampus jayakari)

Male seahorses give birth! In this species, females lay legs that are then carried in a brood pouch by the males until the young are born.

Green sea turtle
(Chelonia mydas)

Young green sea turtles eat fish eggs and jellyfish, but adults feed on seagrass.

Sailfish *(Istiophorus platypterus)*

The fin on the back of a fish is called a dorsal fin. Early voyagers thought the sailfish's dorsal looked like a ship's sail.

Mauritius weevil
(Syzygops vinsoni)

The eyes of this species are situated on the top of their heads.

West Indian Ocean coelacanth *(Latimeria chalumnae)*

Adult coelacanths turn bright blue and spotty to help camouflage them when hunting.

Common fangtooth
(Anoplogaster cornuta)

These are deep-sea predators that live in complete darkness, 5,000 m (16,400 ft) beneath the surface of the water.

Vampire squid
(Vampyroteuthis infernalis)

The vampire squid's skin contains thousands of special cells that produce light. These function like tiny lightbulbs that flash on and off and are used to frighten away enemies.

Painted frogfish *(Antennarius pictus)*

These fish can change the shade of their skin to camouflage themselves in their surroundings.

Portuguese man o' war
(Physalia physalis)

A Portuguese man o' war looks like a jellyfish but is really a large colony of tiny animals called zooids that live and work together. The name comes from an old word for sailing ships.

Bull shark *(Carcharhinus leucas)*

Aggressive bull sharks can live in both salt and freshwater and can travel up rivers.

NORTH AMERICA

The North American continent includes all three climate zones—tropical, temperate, and polar. This produces an extraordinary variety of habitats, ranging from tropical rain forests in Panama to the snowy tundra of Nunavut in Canada, the closest land to the North Pole.

Canada and the USA are two of the world's biggest countries and both have a long list of animal residents. The undisturbed boreal forests of the north provide a safe environment for species that have disappeared farther south. The desert lands on the USA/Mexican border are home to highly specialized animals that can only survive in this dry environment. Like much wildlife, some North American animals are learning to live close to humans. They have moved into towns and changed their habits to take advantage of new feeding opportunities.

The warm seas of Baja and the Caribbean are important feeding grounds for some critically endangered animals. A healthy ocean has a major effect on the number of species living on nearby land. Costa Rica is not large but it has the highest biodiversity of any country on Earth, with more than 500,000 recorded species. It has coastlines on both the Pacific Ocean and the Caribbean Sea. The land in between has forests, national parks, and wetlands.

1 *CANADIAN ARCTIC TUNDRA*

Cold, dry, and very windy, most tundra is found in the Arctic. Animals here have to make the most of the short summers and long winters.

2 *NORTH AMERICA Monarch butterfly*

The striking orange, black, and white hues of the monarch butterfly are a warning to predators that they are poisonous and very bad to eat.

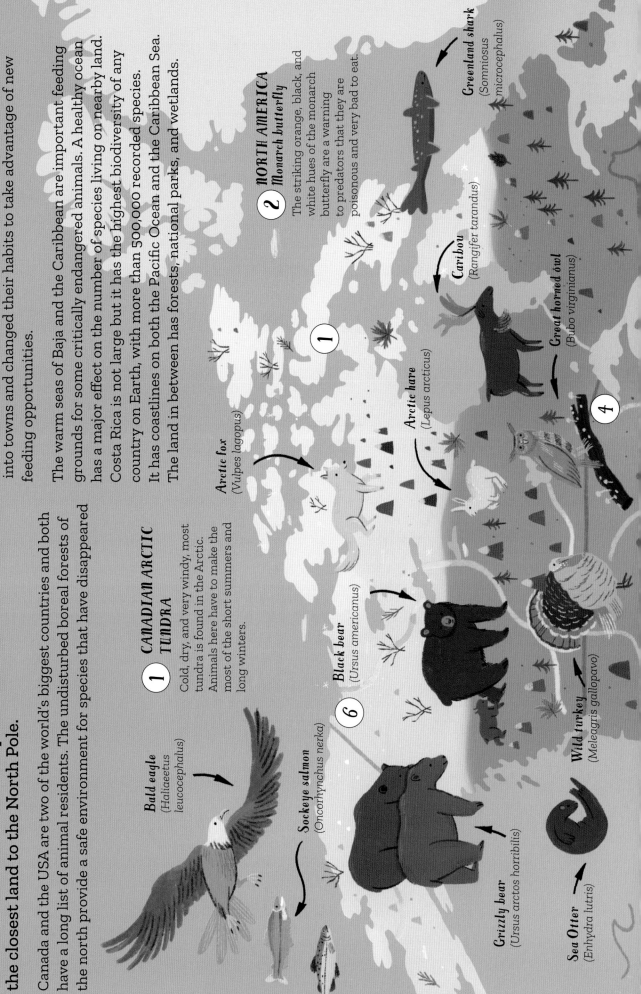

Bald eagle
(*Haliaeetus leucocephalus*)

Sockeye salmon
(*Oncorhynchus nerka*)

Grizzly bear
(*Ursus arctos horribilis*)

Sea Otter
(*Enhydra lutris*)

Black bear
(*Ursus americanus*)

Wild turkey
(*Meleagris gallopavo*)

Arctic fox
(*Vulpes lagopus*)

Arctic hare
(*Lepus arcticus*)

Caribou
(*Rangifer tarandus*)

Great horned owl
(*Bubo virginianus*)

Greenland shark
(*Somniosus microcephalus*)

Snapping turtle
(*Chelydra serpentina*)

Monarch butterfly
(*Danaus plexippus*)

Honduran white bat
(*Ectophylla alba*)

Scarlet ibis
(*Eudocimus ruber*)

(2)

(9)

Giant centipede
(*Scolopendra gigantea*)

Black-tailed prairie dog
(*Cynomys ludovicianus*)

Greater roadrunner
(*Geococcyx californianus*)

(8)

(3)

(7)

Mountain Lion
(*Puma concolor*)

Baja

Western banded gecko
(*Coleonyx variegatus*)

Violet sabrewing
(*Campylopterus hemileucurus*)

Western diamondback rattlesnake
(*Crotalus atrox*)

Turkey vulture
(*Cathartes aura*)

Black widow spider
(*Latrodectus hesperus*)

Bighorn sheep
(*Ovis canadensis*)

(5)

Gray (Grey) whale
(*Eschrichtius robustus*)

(5) CALIFORNIA COAST
Sea otters and kelp

The tangled kelp forests are home to colonies of playful sea otters. The otters help conserve the forests by hunting animals that eat the young kelp.

(8) CENTRAL AMERICA: COSTA RICA

It is impossible not to gasp when you catch a glimpse of hummingbirds sipping nectar. They are marvels and the more you learn about them, the more exciting they become.

(9) THE CARIBBEAN

The warm and fertile Caribbean Sea and islands are alive with animals and plants. Bright skies, soft waves, and an abundance of food make these thriving habitats.

(7) MEXICO

Baja is a peninsula of ancient desert, shrublands, mountains, and sea. It is probably the best place in the world to spot migrating whales.

(3) CHIHUAHUAN DESERT

Home to over 130 species of mammal and 500 species of birds, many of which are active at dawn and dusk to avoid the hottest parts of the day.

(4) MINNESOTA CONIFEROUS FOREST

Home to black bears, many of the animals that live in the remote forests survive the harsh winters by hibernating or migrating.

(6) ALASKA
Northern Pacific Ocean

Mysterious sockeye salmon power their way upstream from the ocean to spawn in the place of their hatching. Their lives are full of transformations.

ARCTIC TUNDRA

The Canadian Arctic tundra is a vast, cold, treeless plain in the far north. Vegetation is mostly short-rooted low shrubs, mosses, and grasses. In summer, the Sun never sets and in winter it hardly appears above the horizon. It goes dark in November and does not get fully light again until the spring.

Snow goose (*Anser caerulescens*)

Snow geese are summer visitors to the tundra. They arrive in May to build nests on the warming ground. They have up to four chicks and fly south in late August.

Arctic fox (*Vulpes lagopus*)

In winter, the fur—or pelage—lightens to white to help camouflage the fox against the snow.

Atlantic cod (*Gadus morhua*)

Cod were once one of the most numerous fish in the North Atlantic but overfishing has dramatically reduced their population.

Sea urchin
(*Strongylocentrotus pallidus*)

Sea urchins live on the seabed, where they eat seaweed and other algae. They are protected against predators by a coat of sharp spines.

Greenland shark
(*Somniosus microcephalus*)

Greenland sharks probably live longer than any other vertebrate species. It is thought that they can reach 400 years old!

Tundra weather is chilly, dry, and very windy. Winters can last for ten months with temperatures of -40°C (-40°F). Summers are short and allow only the top layer of soil to thaw. The earth beneath remains frozen; this is called permafrost.

Few animals live in the tundra all year, and summer brings far more species than winter. Many insects emerge in the short summer, including huge numbers of mosquitoes. These insects are food for migrating birds. When winter returns, the tundra mammals rely on special adaptations to enable them to thrive in this hostile environment.

Ellesmere Island

Arctic Ocean

Victoria Island

Baffin Island

Canadian Arctic Tundra

Caribou (*Rangifer tarandus*)
Caribou and reindeer are the only deer species where both males and females have antlers. They migrate south during the worst of the winter.

Collared pika (*Ochotona collaris*)
Pikas store food for winter by hiding vegetation under rocks.

Red-necked phalarope (*Phalaropus lobatus*)
Unusually, the feathers of female phalaropes are brighter shades than the males.

Arctic hare (*Lepus arcticus*)
Some 20 percent of the Arctic hare's weight is made up of rich body fat. This insulates them against the extreme tundra cold.

MONARCH BUTTERFLY

Monarchs have one of the most amazing lifecycles of any animal. Those in the warm west spend all year in North America. But every autumn, monarchs in the cooler east must migrate south from their breeding grounds to spend winter hibernating in the forests of sunny Mexico.

Black-backed oriole
(Icterus abeillei)
These orioles are one of the few birds that can eat monarch butterflies without becoming ill.

Busy butterflies
Each female monarch butterfly can lay around 1,000 eggs in just a few days.

Feelers
Monarchs have sensory organs in their feet and head that help them identify plants.

Fussy eaters
Monarchs are very picky eaters! Their food plant is milkweed and they need it for survival. This is where females lay their eggs; the leaves provide food for growing caterpillars and the flowers offer nectar for adults.

Fruit snacks
Gardeners feed migrating butterflies by leaving out chunks of sugar-rich watermelon or other ripe fruit to help them refuel.

In spring, the butterflies head back to North America. The journey is around 4,800 km (3,000 mi) and most monarchs only live for around four weeks. This isn't enough time to complete the trip, so instead they stop and breed along the way. Those individuals who set out on the migration will never arrive in the north—but their offspring just might! The adults mate, lay eggs, and then die. The eggs hatch into caterpillars and then change into butterflies that continue the flight north in a kind of relay. This happens three or four times before the migrating monarchs finally reach their summer home.

SUMMER

SUMMER

North America

SPRING

Pacific Ocean

Gulf of Mexico

Atlantic Ocean

Dangers ahead

Migrating butterflies fly quite low to the ground and many are killed by road traffic.

Beware!

The wings of monarch caterpillars are brightly pigmented to warn predators that they contain poison and taste very bad.

A little help

People who care for the butterflies plant milkweed along the route of their flyways.

DESERT

The Chihuahuan Desert spreads from the southwestern United States and crosses the international border into northern Mexico. The word "desert" means an area with very low rainfall. All deserts are dry but they are not all hot. The Chihuahuan Desert is on a high plateau between tall mountain ranges. It can be very cold, especially at night when the temperature often drops to freezing.

American golden eagle
(*Aquila chrysaetos*)
Golden eagles need high cliff ledges to build their huge platform nests.

Bighorn sheep
(*Ovis canadensis*)
The solid curved horns of a male can weigh up to 14 kg (30 lb). They are used to drive away other males and to defend against predators.

Honeypot ant (*Myrmecocystus*)
Honeypot ants store food in their bodies for use when there is nothing to eat. Their abdomens become hugely swollen, making the ants five times their normal size.

Praying mantis
(*Stagmomantis limbata*)
A hunting mantis will wait on a branch for hours with its front legs folded back and ready to strike. They were thought to look like a person kneeling in prayer.

Black-tailed prairie dog
(*Cynomys ludovicianus*)
Prairie dogs are rodents that live in colonies called "towns." These contain a complicated maze of underground tunnels where the animals sleep and give birth.

Western diamondback rattlesnake (*Crotalus atrox*)
The snakes' rattle is produced when it vibrates hard sections of its tail. These are made of keratin, just like fingernails.

Desert black swallowtail butterfly
(*Papilio polyxenes*)
Male swallowtail butterflies have bright yellow patches on their wings. This attracts mates but also means that they are more likely to be seen—and taken by predators—than the less brightly shaded female.

Pronghorn
(*Antilocapra americana*)
Pronghorns are not true antelopes. They are the last living species of a family of grazing animals that is almost extinct.

At very dry times of the year, animals regularly visit the Rio Grande to drink. This river passes through the desert and never dries up. Its water is vitally important to the desert's ecosystem.

The Chihuahuan is the biggest desert in North America and is home to a surprisingly long list of animal species. Some deserts are just sand and rocks but the Chihuahuan is a shrub-desert, meaning it has low-growing plants scattered around the landscape.

USA

Chihuahuan Desert

Mexico

Gila monster
(*Heloderma suspectum*)

These are the only venomous lizards in North America. They are slow-moving and rarely bite humans. Gila monsters eat small mammals, lizards, and insects.

Black-tailed jackrabbit
(*Lepus californicus*)

The jackrabbits' enormous ears have a network of blood vessels that carry heat. The thin ears act like a radiator that allows heat to escape, keeping the animal cool.

Collared peccary
(*Pecari tajacu*)

Collared peccaries live in groups of around 15 and usually eat fruit, roots, and plants.

Mountain lion/cougar
(*Puma concolor*)

Mountain lions hold the record for the animal with the most names in English. There are more than 40, including cougar, puma, red lion, panther, and catamount.

Red-spotted toad
(*Anaxyrus punctatus*)

Red-spotted toads live in rocky parts of the desert.

Greater roadrunner
(*Geococcyx californianus*)

The perfectly named roadrunner can run at up to 32 km/h (20 mph).

CONIFEROUS FORESTS

Minnesota's coniferous forests are cool and moist. The Northwoods, as they are known, contain evergreen trees with fragrant needles that bear cones. Mosquito-filled in summer and deep in snow over winter, these ancient forests are teeming with birdlife. Chickadees, finches, woodpeckers, goshawks, and ravens spend at least some of their year here. Protected by law, the major threats to the forest are tornados and bushfires. This area of Minnesota forms part of the boreal forest, which is the world's largest biome, or community of plants and animals living in a similar climate.

Minnesota is on one of North America's busiest bird migration routes. In autumn, millions of birds fly to the warmer south. At the same time, others arrive from the north to avoid harsh weather in the Arctic. In the spring, many return. By May, the Northwoods' dawn chorus will feature 150 different species. Resident and migrant birds breed quickly to make the most of the short summer.

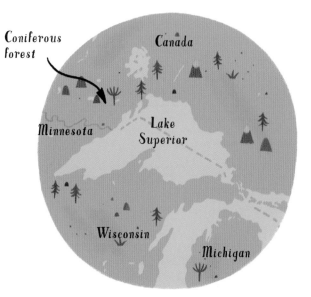

Coniferous forest
Canada
Minnesota
Lake Superior
Wisconsin
Michigan

Great horned owl
(Bubo virginianus)
Great horned owls have a 1.5 m (5 ft) wingspan and can't easily fly through dense forests. They nest on the edge of woodland but hunt in more open areas.

Wild turkey
(Meleagris gallopavo)
At night, turkeys sleep high in the trees, away from predators such as bobcats and coyotes.

Snapping turtle *(Chelydra serpentina)*
Snapping turtles are powerful hunters. They have no teeth but their sharp beaks cut like knives.

American dagger moth caterpillar *(Acronicta americana)*
The caterpillars' long hairs are tipped with a chemical that causes itching and a painful rash when touched.

17-year cicada
(Magicicada cassinii)

Cicada eggs hatch into larvae that burrow into the ground to feed on roots. An astonishing 17 years later, they emerge from the soil, shed their skins, and become winged adults.

Oak treehopper
(Platycostis vittata)

Hoppers feed on the sweet sap beneath the bark of oak trees.

Humboldt's flying squirrel
(Glaucomys oregonensis)

These glide like a paper airplane by stretching out the skin between their front and back legs.

Western tiger salamander
(Ambystoma mavortium)

Adults spend most of their lives underground.

Black bear
(Ursus americanus)

These bears hibernate over winter when food is hard to find.

North American porcupine
(Erethizon dorsatum)

Although the word porcupine means "thorn pig," these animals are rodents. An adult porcupine has around 30,000 sharp quills, which are used for defence and to keep warm.

Fur trade

Sea otters once provided the world's most expensive fur. One hunter killed 1,000 animals in a single year.

Canoe encounter

Sea otters sometimes climb on canoes and rest next to the human rower!

Sleeping safely

Sleeping sea otters spin on the water surface to tangle themselves in kelp. This acts as an anchor and stops them from floating away with the tide.

Protectors of the forest

Sea otters help protect the kelp forests. They hunt for sea urchins that can damage the forest with their huge appetite for kelp.

Floating together

Sea otters are very social and often gather together in groups known as "rafts." Each raft can contain up to 100 otters and they are usually all-female or all-male groups. The animals often link feet so they stay together.

Tool use

Clever sea otters use tools to open shellfish. They float on their back with a flat stone balanced on their stomach. Then they strike the shellfish hard against the stone until the shell cracks open.

California

Santa Cruz
Santa Barbara

Sea otter range

Mexico

SEA OTTER

At a distance, the dark forms bobbing among the kelp look like driftwood. Close up, they transform into a raft of otters tangled together as they play in the water. Sea otters live on the western coast of North America and Canada and spend most of their life in the sea, rarely coming to land. They eat, sleep, and even give birth in the water. Seawater is cool in these areas and the otters need lots of food to provide the energy to keep warm. In a single day, they can eat the equivalent of 40 percent of their own bodyweight. They also have the densest fur of any mammal.

Their coats made them a very popular target for hunters who sold the skins into the fur trade. Thanks to a hunting ban, their population has increased, though they remain an endangered species.

SOCKEYE SALMON

In the icy waters of the Northern Pacific Ocean there lives a fish that is full of surprises. Sockeye salmon are born in freshwater streams. They stay in the area of their birth or "natal habitat" for up to three years. They then journey out to sea, where they grow rapidly, feeding mainly on tiny animals called "zooplankton." They stay in the ocean for between one and four years.

Sea-going sockeyes are called "bluebacks." They have silver sides with black dotting and a bluish top. Then, as they return to their spawning grounds upriver, their bodies turn bright red and their heads become greenish. Males of breeding age develop a humped back and hooked jaws filled with sharp teeth. Males and females both die within a few weeks after spawning. The spawning salmon travel in large groups and create a feeding bonanza for many other animals as they tire.

Grizzly bears
(Ursus arctos) wait on riverbanks to catch and eat salmon swimming upstream.

Upstream swimming
After summer, thousands of adult salmon swim together upstream toward the place where they hatched.

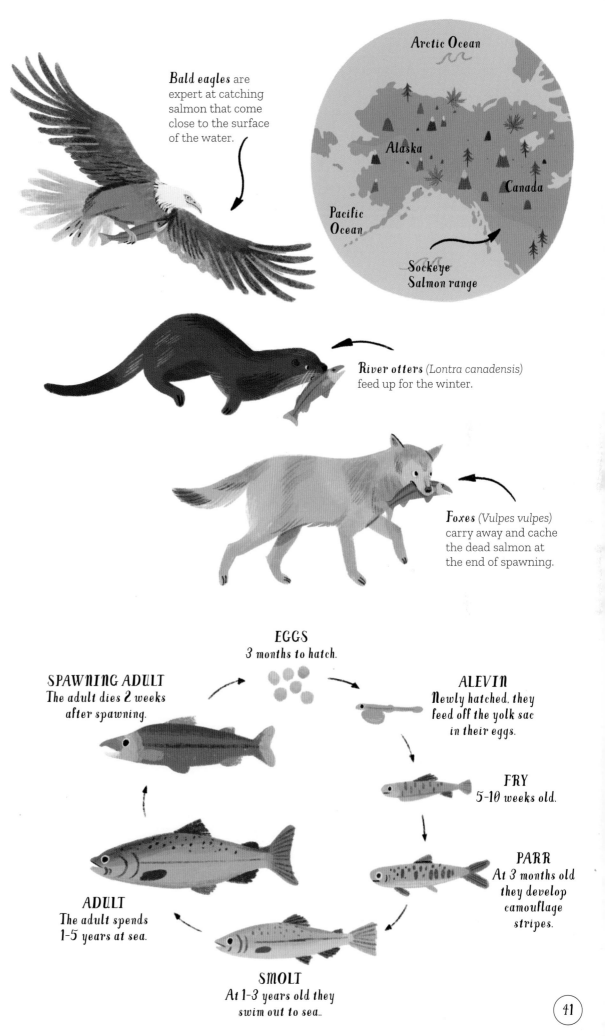

Bald eagles are expert at catching salmon that come close to the surface of the water.

Arctic Ocean

Alaska

Canada

Pacific Ocean

Sockeye Salmon range

River otters (*Lontra canadensis*) feed up for the winter.

Foxes (*Vulpes vulpes*) carry away and cache the dead salmon at the end of spawning.

EGGS
3 months to hatch.

SPAWNING ADULT
The adult dies 2 weeks after spawning.

ALEVIN
Newly hatched, they feed off the yolk sac in their eggs.

FRY
5-10 weeks old.

PARR
At 3 months old they develop camouflage stripes.

ADULT
The adult spends 1-5 years at sea.

SMOLT
At 1-3 years old they swim out to sea..

BAJA PENINSULA

United States of America

Mexico

Gulf of California

Pacific Ocean

Baja

Step back in time in the Baja Peninsula. Here, vultures rest on huge cacti, snakes weave across lonely roads, and thousands of wading birds search the beaches for food. Much of the Baja Peninsuala's dry landscape looks exactly as it did 10,000 years ago. The climate is hot—only in the mountains is it cooler and wetter.

Baja is a long, thin peninsula that is separated from most of Mexico by the Sea of Cortez, a gulf of the Pacific Ocean. These clear, turquoise waters are known as the world's aquarium. The gulf is home to approximately one third of the world's sea mammal species and is possibly the very best place to see whales close up during their migrations. December to April is the whale-watching season. Humpbacks, fin, blue, sei, and minke whales are all possible spots. Baja has become a popular ecotourism destination.

Quino checkerspot
(Euphydryas editha quino)
These extraordinary butterflies have adapted to habitat loss and climate change by moving to cooler, higher altitudes. They have even adopted new food plants.

Long-billed curlew *(Numenius americanus)*
Their long, thin beaks probe deep mud looking for food. The sensitive beak tip can feel the movements of small creatures hidden there.

Black-bellied slider
(Trachemys nebulosa)
Turtles can sometimes be seen sunbathing next to freshwater. If they are disturbed, they slide away quickly into the water— which is how they got their name!

Gray (grey) whale
(Eschrichtius robustus)

The warm water of the Baja Peninsula is the breeding ground for gray (grey) whales. Visitors on small boats are able to view the whales at close range.

Turkey vulture *(Cathartes aura)*

This vulture's name comes from the belief that their red, bald heads look just like those of the male turkey.

Western banded gecko
(Coleonyx variegatus)

These nocturnal reptiles often hunt close to street lamps. They feed on moths and other insects attracted by the artificial light.

Black skimmer *(Rynchops niger)*

Skimmers fly low over the sea with the lower part of the beak slicing through the water. When it touches a fish, the beak closes quickly and snaps up its meal.

Variable sand snake
(Chilomeniscus stramineus)

These small snakes find their prey under the surface of the sand. They are not often seen, but it is possible to spot the sand moving as they hunt.

Black widow spider
(Latrodectus hesperus)

Black widows can be identified by the bright red hour-glass shape on their abdomens.

Violet sabrewing (*Campylopterus hemileucurus*)
Hummingbirds can be very confident and will defend their food supply against much larger animals. The violet sabrewing has even been known to drive off hawks.

White-necked jacobin
(*Florisuga mellivora*)
Jacobins are usually found high in the trees, feeding in the canopy.

Weak legs
Hummingbird legs are not strong. They can hold on to branches but are unable to walk or hop.

Wine-throated hummingbird
(*Selasphorus ellioti*)
Male hummingbirds have iridescent feathers, which means that they are luminous and seem to shift colour with the light.

Good mothers
Female hummingbirds take care of the chicks. They are fed on nectar and small insects.

HUMMINGBIRDS

Everything about hummingbirds is exceptional. They are the most eye-catching of all birds with their iridescent feathers and can eat twice their own weight every day. The bee hummingbird is the world's smallest bird; it weighs the same as a paperclip!

Humans have a heart rate of approximately 70 beats per minute while a hummingbird's is 1,250! A hummingbird at rest breathes in and out 250 times every minute and even faster when flying.

Hummingbirds beat their wings faster than any other species—up to 200 beats per second. Their name comes from the whirring sound made by their rapidly moving wings. Lots of people call them "hummers."

There are around 350 hummingbird species. Most stay around the warm tropics but a few species migrate to breeding grounds in the spring. The Rufus hummingbird flies 6,400 km (4,000 mi) every year from Mexico to Alaska and back again.

Eyelash viper
(Bothriechis schlegelii)
Tiny eyelash vipers hunting in trees are one of the few predators that will target fast-moving hummingbirds.

Atlantic Ocean

Central America

Hummingbirds live throughout central America.

Pacific Ocean

Rufous-crested coquette
(Lophornis delattrei)
Male and female hummingbirds do not have similar plumage. Females have les bright feathers than males. This means they are better hidden when on the nest.

Resting
At night, hummingbirds do not sleep, instead they go into torpor. Their heart rate slows and their temperature drops. This helps them conserve energy.

Eating their fill
Hummingbirds feed mainly on energy-rich nectar from flowers. Artificial nectar in special feeders can attract hundreds of birds, who flock to take advantage of this food supply.

Green violetear
(Colibri thalassinus)
Male hummers use their bright feathers to attract a mate.

Plain-capped starthroat
(Heliomaster constantii)
Most hummers feed on flying insects whenever possible.

Aerial acrobatics
Hummingbirds are the only birds that can fly upside down, backward, and sideways.

Nesting
Hummingbird females usually lay two eggs in their nest.

THE CARIBBEAN

Every magnificent Caribbean island is unique. From sandy beaches and aquamarine seas to lush interiors alive with plants and animals, each one is made distinct by temperature, rainfall, and terrain. The Caribbean Sea and islands are listed as a biodiversity hotspot, which is an area that contains an amazing range of endemic species but is also threatened by human activity.

Introduced species are a concern on some islands. Monkeys, mongooses, and giant African snails have all been released in certain areas. They hunt local species or compete for food supplies and each has a major impact on the habitat.

Much of the Caribbean's iconic wildlife can't be found anywhere else. That can be a conservation problem because islands have limited space and animals have nowhere to move to if a habitat is destroyed. Many islands are now nature reserves. International efforts are being made to protect these sensitive ecosystems.

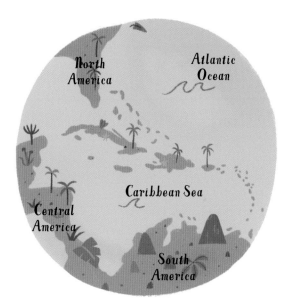

Scarlet ibis
(Eudocimus ruber)
Scarlet ibis live in huge flocks. At night, there are often 25,000 birds roosting in the Coroni Swamp on Trinidad.

Christmas tree worm
(Spirobranchus giganteus)
These marine worms feed by catching tiny creatures in their fan-like arms that look exactly like a decorated Christmas tree.

Giant centipede
(Scolopendra gigantea)
These predators can reach 25 cm (10 in) long. They have a very venomous bite that rarely kills humans but is always extremely painful.

Union Island gecko
(Gonatodes daudini)
These are extremely rare; they live in just one small forest on one small island. The population is falling fast because poachers sell them to the exotic pet trade.

Solenodon *(Solenodon paradoxus)*
A solenodon has a ball-and-socket joint on its long nose bone. The nose can twist and turn just like a human shoulder.

Spiny orb spider (*Gasteracantha cancriformis*)
Spiders kill prey with venom that also turns the inside of the insect's body to liquid. Spiders eat by sucking the liquefied prey through a long thin tube—a little like sucking soup through a straw!

Hispaniolan trogon
(*Priotelus roseigaster*)
These birds constantly change the volume of their calls, which makes it difficult to pinpoint their location.

Honduran white bat
(*Ectophylla alba*)
These clever animals are also called tent-making bats. They cut plant stems so the leaves fold down and create perfect little shelters that look exactly like tents.

Desmarest's hutia
(*Capromys pilorides*)
These shy rodents live on the island of Cuba and have a slow, waddling walk.

Saint Vincent parrot
(*Amazona guildingii*)
This parrot has been adopted as the bird of St. Vincent because its feathers are yellow, blue, and green— the same as the national flag.

Antiguan racer (*Alsophis antiguae*)
Antiguan racers are one the world's rarest snakes. Their numbers have been reduced by mongooses and rats.

SOUTH AMERICA

The mighty Amazon River is the pulse of South America. The river is the heart of the vast Amazon rain forest—the largest tropical rain forest on Earth. This complex ecosystem is home to an extraordinary range of wildlife. But this is just one of the continent's rich and varied habitats, each providing a home to specialized wildlife. Rain forest animals could never survive on the cold, windswept slopes of the Andes or in the open grasslands of Paraguay, where trees are rare. Each environment supplies a unique combination of shelter, food, water, and temperature. Most species have evolved to live in just one kind of habitat.

The idea that animals adapted and evolved according to their environment was triggered by a visit to the Galápagos Islands by Charles Darwin in 1835. He discovered reptile and bird species that had originally lived on mainland South America but had changed to thrive in their new island habitat. The Galápagos are still one of the best places in which to view animals at close range.

All 12 South American countries have introduced conservation projects designed to protect threatened habitats and wildlife. Sixty years ago, whales were becoming a rare sight in the southern Atlantic. But after commercial hunting was banned in these waters, the population started to recover. Today, the southern Atlantic waters are home to 51 species of whales and dolphins.

Scarlet macaw
(Ara macao)

Giant river otter
(Pteronura brasiliensis)

Hercules beetle
(Dynastes hercules)

Red howler monkey
(Alouatta puruensis)

Jaguar
(Panthera onca)

Amazon rain forest

Piranha
(Pygocentrus species)

Harpy eagle
(Harpia harpyja)

Leptogenys ant
(Leptogenys species)

Tamandua
(Tamandua tetradactyla)

Marine iguana
(Amblyrhynchus cristatus)

Great frigatebird
(Fregata minor)

Giant manta ray
(Manta birostris)

Spectacled caiman
(Caiman crocodilus)

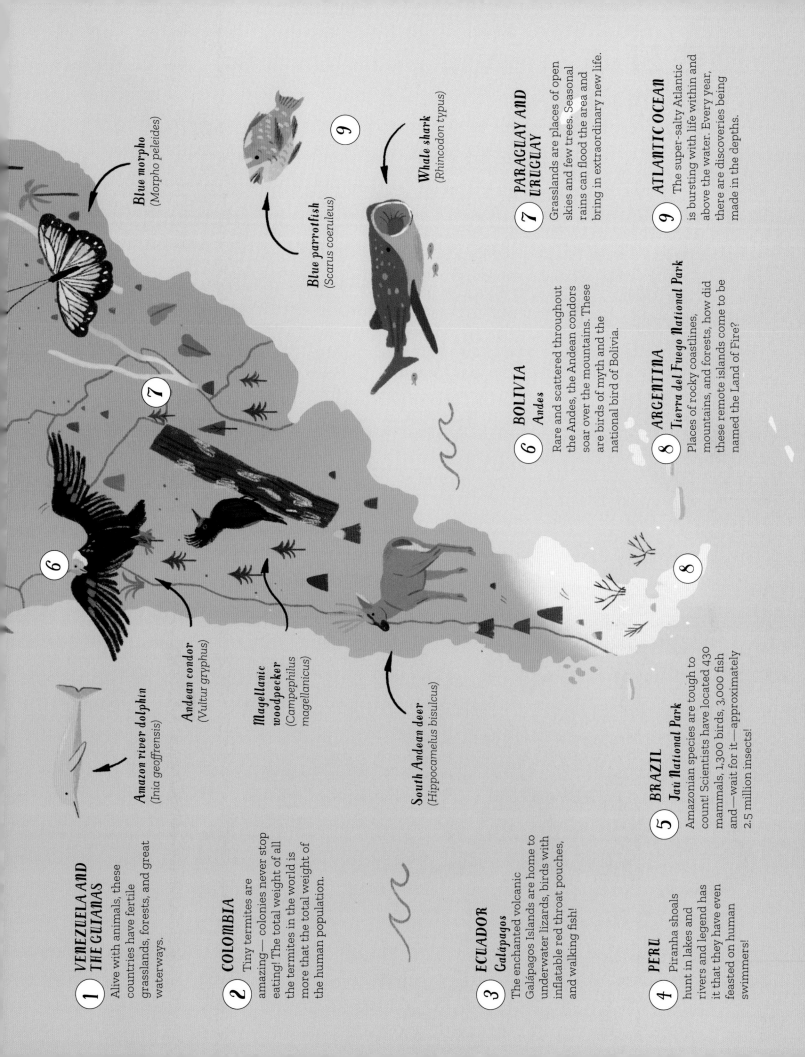

Blue morpho
(Morpho peleides)

9

Blue parrotfish
(Scarus coeruleus)

Whale shark
(Rhincodon typus)

7 **PARAGUAY AND URUGUAY**
Grasslands are places of open skies and few trees. Seasonal rains can flood the area and bring in extraordinary new life.

9 **ATLANTIC OCEAN**
The super-salty Atlantic is bursting with life within and above the water. Every year, there are discoveries being made in the depths.

6 **BOLIVIA**
Andes
Rare and scattered throughout the Andes, the Andean condors soar over the mountains. These are birds of myth and the national bird of Bolivia.

8 **ARGENTINA**
Tierra del Fuego National Park
Places of rocky coastlines, mountains, and forests, how did these remote islands come to be named the Land of Fire?

7

6

8

Andean condor
(Vultur gryphus)

Amazon river dolphin
(Inia geoffrensis)

Magellanic
woodpecker
(Campephilus
magellanicus)

South Andean deer
(Hippocamelus bisulcus)

1 **VENEZUELA AND THE GUIANAS**
Alive with animals, these countries have fertile grasslands, forests, and great waterways.

2 **COLOMBIA**
Tiny termites are amazing— colonies never stop eating! The total weight of all the termites in the world is more that the total weight of the human population.

3 **ECUADOR**
Galápagos
The enchanted volcanic Galápagos Islands are home to underwater lizards, birds with inflatable red throat pouches, and walking fish!

4 **PERU**
Piranha shoals hunt in lakes and rivers and legend has it that they have even feasted on human swimmers!

5 **BRAZIL**
Jaú National Park
Amazonian species are tough to count! Scientists have located 430 mammals, 1,300 birds, 3,000 fish and—wait for it—approximately 2.5 million insects!

VENEZUELA and the GUIANAS

The Guianas are treasures tucked away on the northeast side of South America. They are three different countries: Suriname, French Guiana, and Guyana. The word Guiana means "land of many waters." Together with Venezuela, they make up one of the world's most biodiverse regions. More than 3,000 vertebrate animal species have been recorded here, including some of South America's most endangered animals.

The climate of all four countries includes both high temperatures and rainfall. The rainy season results in seasonal flooding, and many of the animals have evolved to live either in the water or up in the trees. Around half of the land is forested. A high percentage of the forest is protected by a series of national parks, where hunting and logging are banned. The human population is low so the forests do not face the same threats from agriculture as those in other areas of the tropics.

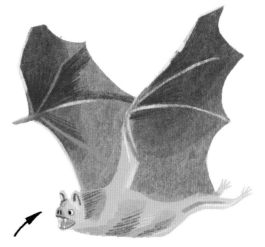

Common vampire bat (*Desmodus rotundus*)
These bats are no suckers! Rather than suck blood from their prey, they make a small scrape in an animal's skin and lap up the blood that seeps out.

Surinam toad
(*Pipa pipa*)
These extraordinary toads grow their young on their backs! The female lays eggs that sink into depressions in the skin on her back. The skin closes over the eggs and eventually tiny frogs emerge.

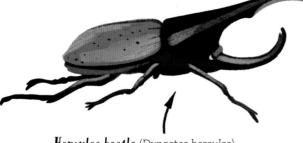

Hercules beetle (*Dynastes hercules*)
Super-strong Hercules beetles can lift up to 100 times their own bodyweight.

Matamata turtle
(*Chelus fimbriata*)
These turtles have a knobbly, rough shell that looks exactly like a rotting log. This camouflages them in the water as they wait to catch and eat passing fish.

Yapok (*Chironectes minimus*)
Yapoks are also known as water opossums. They hunt for small animals in rivers and lakes.

Hoatzin
(*Opisthocomus hoazin*)
Poor fliers, hoatzins eat leaves and flowers that they find by climbing among the trees.

Leafcutter ant *(Atta colombica)*

These ants are farmers! They take leaves underground and chew them into a soft pulp. This is a fertilizer used to grow fungus that provides the ants' food.

Atlantic Ocean

Venezuela

Guyana

Suriname

French Guiana

Water basilisk
(Basiliscus basiliscus)

These lizards literally run on water! Their low bodyweight, high speed, and wide toes stop them from sinking below the surface.

Harpy eagle
(Harpia harpyja)

Harpy eagles catch monkeys and sloths in the treetops.

Goliath bird-eating tarantula
(Theraphosa blondi)

Despite their name, bird-eating spiders feed mainly on insects.

Giant river otter *(Pteronura brasiliensis)*

Giant otters once lived in many South American wetlands. Healthy populations are now found only in the Guianas' forests.

Leptogenys ant
(*Leptogenys* species)

Termites look like ants but the two groups are not related. Leptogenys ants are specialist termite hunters.

White-fringed antwren
(*Formicivora grisea*)

Termites are an important part of the antwrens' diet. Living close to termite nests guarantees a non-stop food supply.

Fungi

Like termites, fungi are agents of decay that break down wood so its nutrients can be recycled.

COLOMBIA

Termites might be among the smallest animals in a rain forest, but they are also some of the most important. Soil in a rain forest is nutritionally poor. Most of the habitat's nutrients and minerals are locked up in the giant trees. They stay there until the tree dies and rots, then the nutrients are absorbed into the ground and are quickly taken up by other plants. But giant trees take many years to decompose without help: cue termites! Termites eat dead wood and their droppings return life-giving nutrients back to the soil, which are then used by all nearby plants. One termite alone cannot eat enough wood to make a difference but rain forests contain literally billions of them, of very many species. Termite nests are often very close to each other and they will often fight over territory. Termites may be small and blind but without them, rain forests as we know them could not exist.

Golden poison frog
(*Phyllobates terribilis*)

The most poisonous animal on Earth, one frog contains enough poison to kill ten humans, but all they eat are termites and ants.

Towering nests

A termite nest on the ground can be 3 m (10 ft) tall and contain an amazing 2 million termites.

Pacific Ocean

Venezuela

Colombia

Ecuador

Brazil

Peru

Giant armadillo
(Priodontes maximus)

Giant armadillos use strong, curved claws to rip open termite nests. They weigh up to 35 kg (75 lb) and can eat an entire colony in one night.

Tamandua
(Tamandua tetradactyla)

Some termite species build nests high in the trees, where they are eaten by small, agile tamanduas. They don't have teeth but they don't need them as tiny termites can be swallowed whole.

53

Great frigatebird
(Fregata minor)

Male frigatebirds have a stretchy patch of skin under the throat that expands like a red balloon. This is used to attract mates in the breeding season.

Galapagos Islands

Pacific Ocean

Flightless cormorant
(Phalacrocorax harrisi)

These cormorants have lost the ability to fly because the islands have no large predators and food is plentiful.

Giant manta ray
(Manta birostris)

Scientists do not know why giant manta rays jump high out of the sea. They might be communicating with other rays, or they could be trying to dislodge the parasites that cling to their bodies.

Sea lion
(Zalophus wollebaeki)

Sea lion or seal? Sea lions can be recognized by their small ears, while seals' ears are hidden under their fur.

Green warbler finch *(Certhidea olivacea)*

Green warblers belong to a group called Darwin's finches. Each species has a different-shaped beak that is best suited for the food supply on their home island.

GALÁPAGOS ISLANDS

The Galápagos Islands are part of Ecuador. They are 1,000 km (620 mi) from the coast of South America and are famous as the place that inspired Charles Darwin's theory of evolution. There are more than 100 islands. These are located directly above giant undersea volcanoes that occasionally erupt. Birds can fly to the Galápagos Islands, but it is difficult for other animals to reach them.

Reptiles and invertebrates probably arrived on floating logs from the South American mainland. Bats and rice rats (*Aegialomys galapagoensis*) are the only native land mammals on the islands. Hunting is banned in the Galápagos Islands, and the animals have become extremely comfortable around people. One sea lion regularly shelters inside the town's bank to avoid the hot sun.

Most of the landscape is closed to humans. There is a small network of footpaths for visitors to explore, but everything else is for wildlife only.

Galápagos penguin
(*Spheniscus mendiculus*)

Life on the Equator would be much too hot for the penguins without the cold Antarctic waters that flow up to the islands.

Marine iguana
(*Amblyrhynchus cristatus*)

Marine iguanas are descendants of forest lizards from South America. They evolved into a new species that lives on the shore and eats seaweed.

Sally Lightfoot crab
(*Grapsus grapsus*)

These crabs live on almost every Galápagos beach.

Lava gull (*Leucophaeus fuliginosus*)

These live only on the Galápagos Islands and are the world's rarest gull, with a total population of around 500 birds.

PIRANHA

Piranhas have a truly gruesome reputation that they really don't deserve. In movies, they are often portrayed as killer fish that attack on sight and strip bodies clean in just a few minutes. In fact, many fish species are hunters and piranhas perform a useful role as scavengers that clean up the rivers and stop diseases from spreading.

Piranhas will kill live animals but most of the time they eat water invertebrates and carrion—that is, animals that are already dead. They only hunt live food when there is nothing else to eat. Piranha attacks on humans are extremely rare. Most involve just a quick nibble of a toe in the water!

Traditionally, piranhas form an important part of the diet of indigenous peoples, who also use the piranhas' sharp teeth as cutting tools. They catch the piranha by baiting it with a small piece of meat suspended in the water.

Cocoi heron
(Ardea cocoi)
Cocoi herons cannot chew. Instead, they swallow piranhas whole.

Spectacled caiman
(Caiman crocodilus)
Spectacled caiman are the piranhas' most frequent predator.

Red-bellied piranha
(Pygocentrus nattereri)
There are many species of piranha. Red-bellieds live in large groups called shoals as protection against predators.

Piranha teeth
Piranha teeth are triangular and pointed. The edges are razor-sharp. In the local Tupi language, *piranha* means "biting-fish."

A numbers game
Female piranhas lay up to 5,000 eggs but only a few survive to adulthood.

Gone fishing
People living in the Amazon rain forest catch piranhas with a strong piece of twine and a hook.

Tasting talents
Piranhas can taste blood in the water from up to 3 km (2 mi) away.

Brazil

Pacific Ocean

Peru

Other species of piranha include almost vegetarian *camunani* (*Tometes camunani*) and the **redeye piranha** (*Serrasalmus rhombeus*). The bite of this fish is more powerful than that of any shark!

Feeding Frenzy
Piranhas will fight among themselves when they find a dead animal in the water. This is called a feeding frenzy.

Amazon river dolphin
(*Inia geoffrensis*)
Amazon River dolphins are pink and live in freshwater. Piranhas form a large part of their diet.

57

JAÚ NATIONAL PARK

In the heart of the Amazon is the Jaú National Park. This is the largest rain forest reserve in South America. It protects a habitat and wildlife that are severely threatened in other parts of the continent. Rain forests are home to 50 percent of all land species known on Earth but cover only 2 percent of the planet's surface.

Daily rainfall, seasonal flooding, humidity, and warmth combine to create the most complicated of all land habitats. It helps to think of rain forests as existing in layers. Wildlife lives in different heights of the forest. Animals such as ants, termites, and slugs often live on the forest floor. The next layer up is the undercanopy, which gets more light and is home to small birds, tree frogs, butterflies, and monkeys. The canopy is the roof of the forest where sloths live and feed. Finally, there is the emergent layer of the tallest trees, where eagles and large birds can be found.

Three-toed sloth
(Bradypus variegatus)

Sloths move slowly. Their average speed is just 240 m (787 ft) an hour!

Red howler monkey
(Alouatta puruensis)

Howlers are LOUD! They defend territories with a series of howls that can be heard 5 km (3 mi) away. These are the loudest calls made by any land animal.

Jaguar *(Panthera onca)*

Jaguars are apex predators of the Amazon; no other animal is a threat to them.

Peanut-head bug
(Fulgora laternaria)

When threatened, they open their wings to show the eyespots that make them look like much bigger animals.

Giant damselfly
(Megaloprepus caerulatus)

Hunting in the undercanopy, damselflies eat the large spiders that build their webs between branches.

Scarlet macaw (*Ara macao*)

Macaws are one of the most intelligent of all birds.

Lichen katydid
(*Markia hystrix*)

Katydids are great at disguise! They are camouflaged to hide among the mosses and lichen that thrive in a rain forest.

Pygmy marmoset
(*Cebuella pygmaea*)

These tiny primates scrape holes in the bark of rain forest trees and eat the sugary sap inside.

Velvet worm (*Onychophora* species)

Velvet worms live on the damp rain forest floor.

Sabre-Tooth Longhorn Beetle
(*Macrodontia cervicornis*)

These beetles spend ten years as white larvae, eating the soft wood of dead trees.

Blue morpho
(*Morpho peleides*)

Morpho butterflies' wings are 20 cm (8 in) wide. Their bright blue scales reflect the Sun and frighten away predators.

Gliding spider
(*Selenops*)

Many rain forest spiders live in the treetops. Some have a very flat body that allows them to glide long distances through the air.

Venezuela

Colombia

Peru

Jaú
National
Park

Bolivia

Brazil

ANDES' CONDORS

The wingspan of a condor is approximately the length of a small car! Powered flight is not easy for condors because they are so heavy. Their massive wings act like kites: the birds are carried by the wind and warm air currents. They often soar to 5.5 km (3.5 mi) high in the sky and use superb eyesight to search for food in the landscape below.

Spreading their wings
A condor's wingspan is approximately twice an adult human's arm span.

Feeding young
Young condors stay with their parents for around a year before leaving to find their own territory.

Easy identification
Released condors are fitted with numbered tags on their wings so they can be identified from a distance.

In flight
Condors ride air currents and can cover more than 300 km (180 mi) a day.

Baldies
Condors are bald. Their featherless heads are easier to clean after feasting inside the body cavity of a dead animal.

Earth-bound babies
Young condors cannot fly until they are six months old.

Condors are scavengers: they eat animals like cattle and sheep that have died in the mountains. Condors are equipped with powerful beaks that can cut through flesh, but they cannot catch their own food. Birds of prey kill with strong, sharp talons, but condors have surprisingly weak feet. They occasionally catch live animals with their beak but only take small species such as insects and rodents. Condors were in danger of extinction but are now being bred in captivity and released into the wild. Their population is growing.

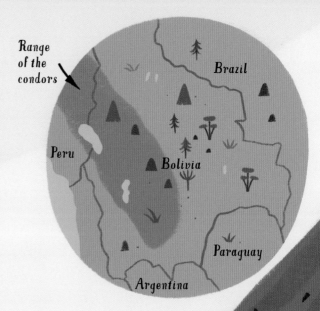

Range of the condors

Peru

Brazil

Bolivia

Paraguay

Argentina

Slow release
Before being released, captive-bred condors are kept in cages in the mountains. This allows them to feel at home in their new surroundings.

Feasting together
Like many scavengers, condors often feed together in groups.

Attracting attention
Male condors have a ridge of pink skin over their beak that can become bright red during the breeding season.

PARAGUAY and URUGUAY

The lowlands of Paraguay and Uruguay are home to wide, wild landscapes and big skies. On these hot, open plains animals can be seen over great distances. There are huge areas with only the occasional tree or shrub. The few forests are found on damp riverbanks. Central to the plain are hundreds of different grass species. This is called the savannah.

Savannahs thrive in warm areas that have a rainy and a dry season. Heavy rainfall creates floods that provide rich wet habitats inside a dry environment. These are breeding grounds for some animals and drinking holes for others. Today, South American grasslands are used to graze cattle. These are not native to South America—they were introduced from Europe about 350 years ago. Farm animals now live alongside wildlife but cattle numbers are growing and might threaten the survival of wild grassland animals.

Black spine-neck swamp turtle (*Acanthochelys spixii*)
Males feed at the edge of pools, while females feed in the middle. This guarantees that they do not compete for food.

Capybara
(*Hydrochoerus hydrochaeris*)
These are the biggest rodents in the world and can be the size of large dogs.

Cuyaba dwarf frog
(*Physalaemus nattereri*)
When viewed from behind, this frog appears to have huge eyes on its bottom! These false eyes are markings on the skin that make a predator think it is approaching a much larger animal.

Giant anteater
(*Myrmecophaga tridactyla*)
The anteater's tongue flicks in and out up to 150 times a minute as it licks up ants from their nest.

Yellow anaconda
(Eunectes notaeus)
Anacondas coil around their prey tightly to suffocate it.

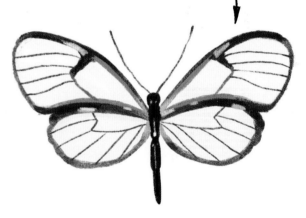

Pacific Ocean

Paraguay

Atlantic Ocean

Uruguay

Crested screamer
(Chauna torquata)
True to their name, these birds produce an extremely loud scream that sounds a little like a badly played trumpet!

Clearwing butterfly
(Episcada hymenaea)
Their transparent wings make clearwings very difficult to see against the undergrowth.

Streamer-tailed tyrant
(Gubernetes yetapa)
The tail of the tyrant is twice the length of its body.

Maned wolf
(Chrysocyon brachyurus)
These elegant wolves are largely vegetarian. They eat wolf apples, the fruit of a small tree.

Austral parakeet
(Enicognathus ferrugineus)
Austral parakeets live farther south and in colder conditions than any other parrot.

Thorn-tailed rayadito
(Aphrastura spinicauda)
Their 12 sharp, stiff, tail feathers look like long spines. They are used to attract mates.

Argentina
Chile
Pacific Ocean
Atlantic Ocean
Tierra del Fuego

Commerson's dolphin
(Cephalorhynchus commersonii)
Most dolphins are great voyagers and cover long distances at sea, but Commerson's stay in the waters around Tierra del Fuego.

Puma
(Puma concolor)
Pumas are solitary hunters that live farther south than any other wild cat.

Ringed kingfisher
(Megaceryle torquata)
Ringed kingfishers have webbed feet and hunt in both the sea and freshwater.

Culpeo *(Lycalopex culpaeus)*
These appear fox-like but are more closely related to wolves and jackals.

Fuegan steamer duck
(Tachyeres pteneres)
Steamer ducks are extremely aggressive and may attack other ducks that enter their territory.

CHILE and ARGENTINA

Tierra del Fuego is a large group of islands at the bottom tip of South America. Half of the islands are in Chile and the rest are in Argentina. The name means "land of fire." It was first used by the Portuguese explorer Ferdinand Magellan, who saw columns of smoke rising all along the coast. He mistook the campfires of Indigenous people for a widespread forest fire.

Tierra del Fuego is cold with a high rainfall. It has a fascinating range of habitats that include rocky coastline, rich beech forests, mountains, and glaciers. Summers are short and winters are windy with temperatures that do not usually fall below freezing. The islands' remoteness and small number of human residents mean wildlife is relatively undisturbed. Shy and rare animal species have a chance to thrive here in the wild landscape, including guanacos (*Lama guanicoe*), Andean condors (*Vultur gryphus*), and Patagonian foxes (*Lycalopex griseus*).

Magellanic woodpecker (*Campephilus magellanicus*)
Magellanic woodpeckers are common in the beech forests. The trees provide grubs to eat and protection from the winter storms.

Fur seal (*Arctocephalus australis*)
All seals have fur but it is much denser on a fur seal. The fur traps air and helps to keep out the cold water of the South Atlantic.

South Andean deer (*Hippocamelus bisulcus*)
South Andean deer have long, curly hair that keeps out heavy rain.

ATLANTIC OCEAN

The Atlantic Ocean is divided into two areas, the North and South. It covers 21 percent of the Earth and contains many large islands. It is the saltiest of the world's oceans, and it also has the busiest shipping lanes. Beneath the waves is a complicated marine ecosystem and landscape that was hidden from us until very recently. Now there are submarines and remote-controlled vehicles that allow us to explore the deep oceans and uncover the animals that live there. The world's longest mountain range, the Mid-Atlantic ridge, is at the bottom of the Atlantic Ocean. Fish, octopuses, and whales swim through valleys and mountaintops far beneath the sea. We have probably discovered less than half of the animal species that live in the deep Atlantic Ocean and new ones are being discovered every year. This is a very exciting time for ocean exploration.

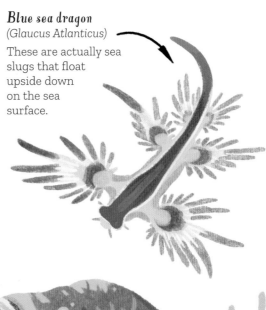

Blue sea dragon
(Glaucus Atlanticus)
These are actually sea slugs that float upside down on the sea surface.

Blue parrotfish
(Scarus coeruleus)
Residents in warm Caribbean waters, these fish have a sharp parrot-like beak that allows them to feed by scraping algae from hard coral.

Atlantic horseshoe crab
(Limulus polyphemus)
The closest relative of the horseshoe crabs are spiders and scorpions.

Arctic tern
(Sterna paradisaea)
These terns fly farther than any other bird—more than 30,000 km (18,641 mi). Every year, they leave their nests in the North Atlantic and fly south to the seas around the Antarctic.

Southern elephant seal *(Mirounga leonina)*
Male elephant seals have loose skin on their nose called a proboscis. This is inflated when the seals fight and was thought to look like the trunk of an elephant.

Sperm whale
(Physeter macrocephalus)
Whales are mammals that need to breathe air, but during a dive they can hold their breath for an hour. Sperm whales eat giant squid deep down in the Atlantic.

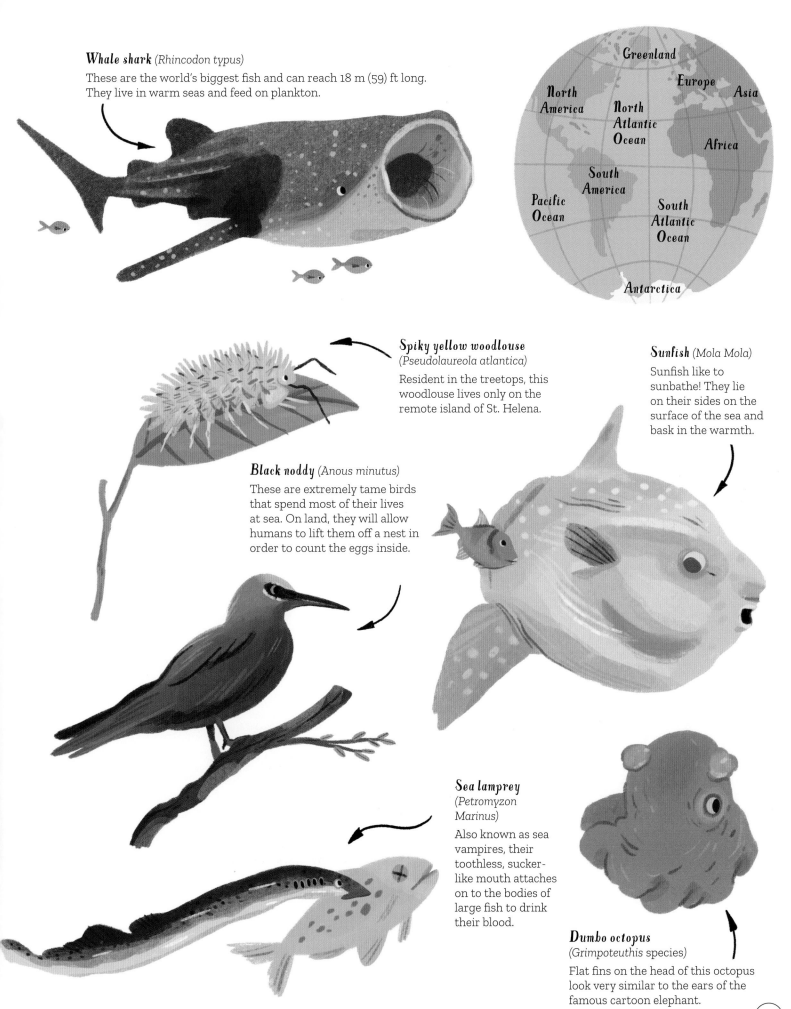

Whale shark (*Rhincodon typus*)
These are the world's biggest fish and can reach 18 m (59) ft long. They live in warm seas and feed on plankton.

Spiky yellow woodlouse
(*Pseudolaureola atlantica*)
Resident in the treetops, this woodlouse lives only on the remote island of St. Helena.

Sunfish (*Mola Mola*)
Sunfish like to sunbathe! They lie on their sides on the surface of the sea and bask in the warmth.

Black noddy (*Anous minutus*)
These are extremely tame birds that spend most of their lives at sea. On land, they will allow humans to lift them off a nest in order to count the eggs inside.

Sea lamprey
(*Petromyzon Marinus*)
Also known as sea vampires, their toothless, sucker-like mouth attaches on to the bodies of large fish to drink their blood.

Dumbo octopus
(*Grimpoteuthis* species)
Flat fins on the head of this octopus look very similar to the ears of the famous cartoon elephant.

ASIA

Almost everything about Asia is record-breaking. It is the world's largest continent and home to more than half of all the people on Earth. The 20 highest mountains are found there, so is the world's lowest area of land—the Dead Sea. The coldest inhabited place on the planet is Oymyakon in Russia—its winter temperature has been recorded down to -67.7 ° C (-90 ° F).

These extremes produce examples of every known wildlife habitat, each with its own unique species. Indonesian rain forests contain very different animals to those living in the Amazonian forests. On the grassland plains of India, wildlife has adapted to seasonal floods. The continent also stimulated some important animal adaptations. The elephant, which is an animal of African grasslands, moved to Asia and became smaller in order to survive in the forests.

One fifth of Asia is made up of islands that have been cut off from the mainland for millions of years. The islands in East Asia are on a very active area of the Earth's crust called the Ring of Fire. It has live volcanoes and earthquakes that mean the islands are still changing and moving, and their animals will continue to evolve with them.

① JAPAN
Central Alps

Trees heavy with snow, steaming-hot pools, and sacred mountains. The Central Alps in winter are simply wild!

② CHINA, MONGOLIA and the KOREAS
Min Mountains or Minshan

The mountains form a natural barrier between busy provinces of China and the Tibetan Plateau. Secretive giant pandas roam the bamboo forest here alongside golden pheasants and dragons!

③ RUSSIA
Kamchatka Peninsula

Kamchatka is dangerous! This is home to tigers, lynx, and eagles—and possibly the world's most beautiful volcano—Kronotsky!

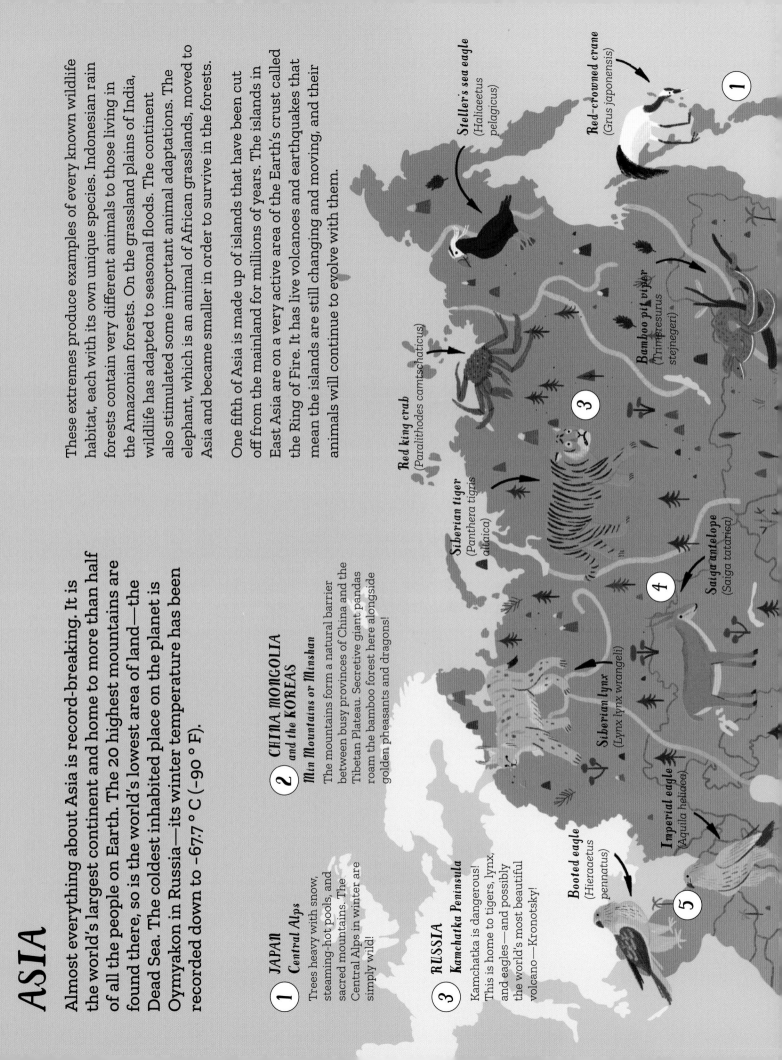

Steller's sea eagle
(*Haliaeetus pelagicus*)

Red-crowned crane
(*Grus japonensis*)

Bamboo pit viper
(*Trimeresurus stejnegeri*)

Red king crab
(*Paralithodes camtschaticus*)

Siberian tiger
(*Panthera tigris altaica*)

Saiga antelope
(*Saiga tatarica*)

Siberian lynx
(*Lynx lynx wrangeli*)

Imperial eagle
(*Aquila heliaca*)

Booted eagle
(*Hieraaetus pennatus*)

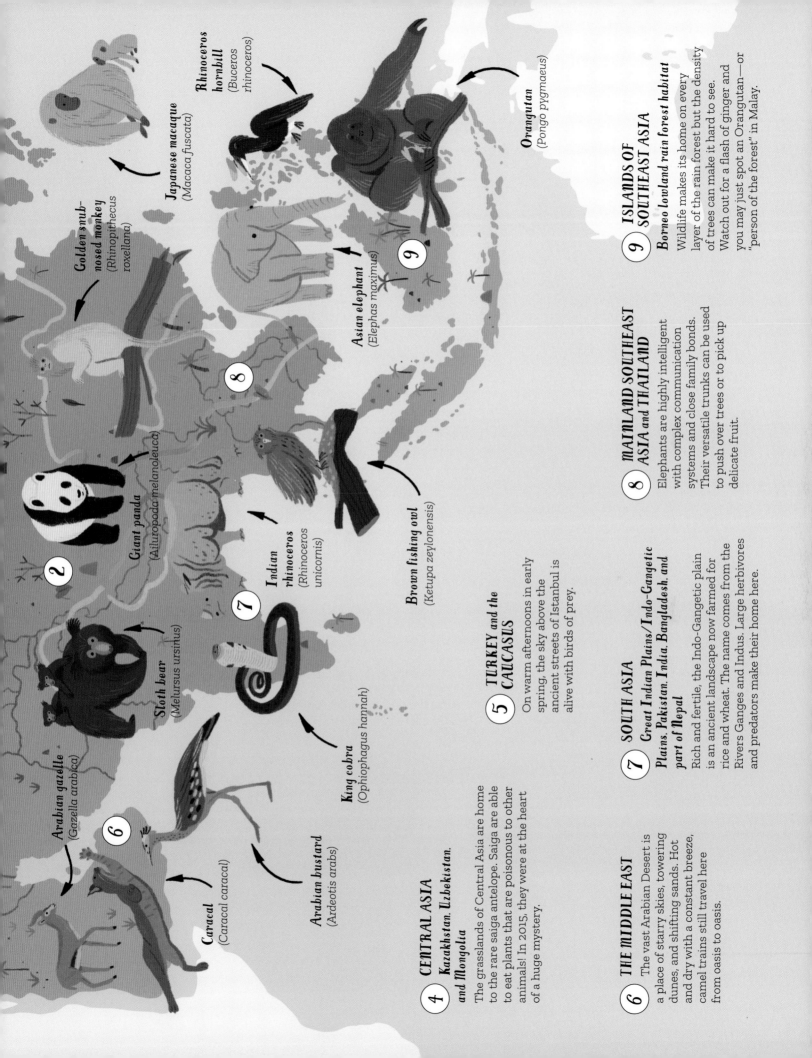

Rhinoceros hornbill
(*Buceros rhinoceros*)

Japanese macaque
(*Macaca fuscata*)

Golden snub-nosed monkey
(*Rhinopithecus roxellana*)

Orangutan
(*Pongo pygmaeus*)

Giant panda
(*Ailuropoda melanoleuca*)

Sloth bear
(*Melursus ursinus*)

Arabian gazelle
(*Gazella arabica*)

Caracal
(*Caracal caracal*)

Arabian bustard
(*Ardeotis arabs*)

King cobra
(*Ophiophagus hannah*)

Indian rhinoceros
(*Rhinoceros unicornis*)

Brown fishing owl
(*Ketupa zeylonensis*)

Asian elephant
(*Elephas maximus*)

4 **CENTRAL ASIA**
Kazakhstan, Uzbekistan, and Mongolia

The grasslands of Central Asia are home to the rare saiga antelope. Saiga are able to eat plants that are poisonous to other animals! In 2015, they were at the heart of a huge mystery.

5 **TURKEY** *and the* **CAUCASUS**

On warm afternoons in early spring, the sky above the ancient streets of Istanbul is alive with birds of prey.

6 **THE MIDDLE EAST**

The vast Arabian Desert is a place of starry skies, towering dunes, and shifting sands. Hot and dry with a constant breeze, camel trains still travel here from oasis to oasis.

7 **SOUTH ASIA**
Great Indian Plains/Indo-Gangetic Plains, Pakistan, India, Bangladesh, and part of Nepal

Rich and fertile, the Indo-Gangetic plain is an ancient landscape now farmed for rice and wheat. The name comes from the Rivers Ganges and Indus. Large herbivores and predators make their home here.

8 **MAINLAND SOUTHEAST ASIA** *and* **THAILAND**

Elephants are highly intelligent with complex communication systems and close family bonds. Their versatile trunks can be used to push over trees or to pick up delicate fruit.

9 **ISLANDS OF SOUTHEAST ASIA**
Borneo lowland rain forest habitat

Wildlife makes its home on every layer of the rain forest but the density of trees can make it hard to see. Watch out for a flash of ginger and you may just spot an Orangutan—or "person of the forest" in Malay.

CENTRAL ALPS

The Japanese Alps are a chain of three mountain ranges that form the spine of Honshu, Japan's largest island. The highest peak is Mount Fuji, a cone-shaped volcano. Summers are warm and sunny but winter in the Alps is long and some places receive more than 12 m (40 ft) of snow every year. Most animals are summer visitors that disappear before the winter. Resident species survive the cold by moving up and down the mountains as the seasons change. They go upward in summer and move back down in winter to avoid the bad weather on the high peaks.

The diverse habitats include grassland, lush valleys, waterways, mixed forests, and scrub. Animals often move between habitats to find shelter and the best sources of food. This is a region of active volcanoes and occasional earthquakes. One of the famous hot springs is in Jigokudani Monkey Park, or "Hell's Valley." This is home to some truly remarkable primates!

Sea of
Japan

North
Pacific
Ocean

Japan

Philippine
Sea

Japanese macaque
(Macaca fuscata)

Mountain monkeys with a taste for the good life spend the icy winters keeping warm in heated pools! The pools are created by natural hot springs from deep within the earth.

Red-crowned crane (Grus japonensis)
Symbols of good luck and long life, these cranes are named for their crimson crowns.

Asian giant hornet (*Vespa mandarinia*)
The largest living hornet has a wingspan of 7.5 cm (3 in).

Japanese giant salamander
(*Andrias japonicus*)
Japanese giant salamanders are amphibians that live in cool, clean streams. Scientists study this increasingly rare species to understand how best to protect them.

Serow (*Capricornis crispus*)
The Japanese government declared these a Special National Monument to protect them from poaching. They are now safe from extinction.

Raccoon dog (*Nyctereutes procyonoides*)
Despite their name and raccoon-like face, their closest relatives are foxes.

Japanese marten (*Martes melampus*)
Their coat or pelage varies from deep brown to dull yellow.

MINSHAN MOUNTAINS

The Minshan Mountains are one of the wildest and least inhabited areas of China.

They are tucked between low-lying farmland and the high, treeless Himalayan mountains. Animals from both zones can be found here. Most of the world's wild pandas live in these mountains and conservation projects to protect them are also helping the other local species. From a distance, the slopes seem to be covered with dense conifer forests, but a closer look shows that in places the undercanopy is made up of huge areas of bamboo. This creates two very different feeding habitats in one place and greatly increases the number of animal species that live here.

Minshan's forests are very steep and often shrouded in fog. There are 18 nature reserves in the mountains and they contain some animal species that have never been closely studied.

Giant panda (*Ailuropoda melanoleuca*)
Fewer than 2,000 individuals now live in China's forests.

Emerald mountain dragon
(*Diploderma iadinum*)
Lizards such as these hibernate during the cold Minshan winters.

Golden snub-nosed monkey
(*Rhinopithecus roxellana*)
The Chinese name for these exquisite blue-faced primates is Sichuan golden hair monkey.

Bamboo pit viper
(*Trimeresurus stejnegeri*)
These snakes have a special organ that detects the body heat of small mammals, allowing them to hunt in the dark.

Firethroat *(Calliope pectardens)*
These birds are said to have the most beautiful song in the Minshan Mountains.

China

Minshan Mountains

South China Sea

Golden pheasant *(Chrysolophus pictus)*
Golden pheasants once lived exclusively in China's forests. They have become very popular in animal collections around the world.

Bamboo partridge *(Bambusicola thoracicus)*
More often heard than seen as they feed on the ground among the dense undergrowth.

Clouded leopard
(Neofelis nebulosa)
These mysterious cats are solitary and nocturnal and spend most of their lives in the treetops.

Chinese three-tailed swallowtail
(Bhutanitis thaidina)
The food plant for the larvae of this rare and little studied species is a climber called Dutchman's pipe *(Aristolochia moupinensis)*.

KAMCHATKA PENINSULA

Kamchatka is a peninsula, an area of land attached to the mainland but surrounded by the sea on three sides. It is the most easterly part of Russia. Kamchatka is wild and mountainous, full of forests surrounded by tundra. There are also 29 active volcanoes here and one, called Maly Semyachik, contains a lake of bright blue acid brought up from inside the volcano.

Steller's sea eagle
(Haliaeetus pelagicus)
Kamchatka is the main breeding area for this eagle.

Siberian tiger
(Panthera tigris altaica)
Critically endangered, there are only around 400 of these tigers left in the wild.

Tufted puffin
(Fratercula cirrhata)
These nest in colonies of up to 30,000 birds.

Siberian lynx
(Lynx lynx wrangeli)
This lynx's furry, webbed feet prevent them from sinking in deep snow.

Harlequin duck
(Histrionicus histrionicus)
These ducks spend spring and summer on freshwater rivers and winter at sea.

Argent and sable moth
(Rheumaptera hastata)
This moth flies during the day and sleeps at night.

Black-capped marmot *(Marmota camtschatica)*
Marmots hibernate for up to eight months each year.

74

Kamchatka is approximately the same size as Sweden and is truly remote. Visitors cannot drive there because there are no roads entering the region. This undisturbed landscape really is a magnificent habitat for wildlife. Indeed, it is one of the most biodiverse habitats in the world and home to the largest population of grizzly bears. The surrounding ocean is rich in fish and other marine species, ideal feeding grounds for much of Kamchatka's wildlife. Even the bears go into the sea to find food.

Arctic Ocean

Bering Sea

Kamchatka Peninsula

Russia

Sea of Okhotsk

Salmon shark
(Lamna ditropis)
Most fish are cold-blooded but this shark produces its own body heat.

Pacific cod
(Gadus macrocephalus)
During the breeding season a female will produce more than 1 million eggs.

Saber-toothed whale
(Mesoplodon stejnegeri)
These whales are named for the long teeth in their lower jaw that stick out like small tusks.

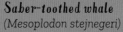

Red king crab
(Paralithodes camtschaticus)
Seabed residents, these crabs have a leg-span up to 1.8 m (5.9 ft).

SAIGA ANTELOPE

Arctic Ocean

Russia

Scandinavia

Central Asia

Indean Ocean

Saiga antelopes are famous for their long-distance migrations. They live in large herds that eat great quantities of grass, which means they need to keep moving to find new feeding grounds. They travel around 1,000 km (620 mi) a year, passing through five countries, crossing roads, and swimming wide rivers. They avoid forests, keeping in the open where they can easily see approaching predators. Males have horns but these don't deter against wolves. The saigas' main protection is their speed.

Fighting off rivals
Males use their horns to fight rivals at the start of the breeding season.

Clever noses
Saiga have inflated noses that help filter out dust kicked up by the rest of the herd. In winter, their noses heat up cold air before it enters the saiga's lungs.

Saiga are a critically endangered species. Millions once covered the grasslands of Central Asia, but 95 percent of the population has disappeared. In 2015, 200,000 saiga died mysterious in just a few days. They had been infected by bacteria in the grass. Emergency conservation projects were created to protect their habitat and cut down on illegal poaching. Females frequently give birth to two calves every year, allowing their population to grow quickly.

Illegal hunting
Saiga are still being killed for their horns. Some people believe they cool fever.

Falling prey to disease
In 2015, a mass die-off event occurred. It was caused by a bacterial infection from grass.

Taking cover
Newly born calves hide in long grass. Just three days later, they are strong enough to run with the adults.

Gray (grey) wolf (Canis lupus)
Wolves are the saigas' main predator. They usually take weak or injured animals. Healthy saiga are too fast to catch.

77

BIRD MIGRATION

European birds often avoid hostile winter weather by flying south to Africa. They then return north to breed in spring. The most important migration route from Africa to Europe is over Turkey. Every spring and summer, millions of birds navigate this flyway to avoid crossing the sea. But why—what makes flight over land more appealing? Put your hand above (not on) a hot radiator and you will feel the heat rising. The Sun warms land much faster than it heats the sea. The warm land then heats the air—and hot air always rises. When small birds fly, they use the strength in their wings to keep them aloft. Larger birds, with greater wingspans, take advantage of the power of warm air currents to help them fly.

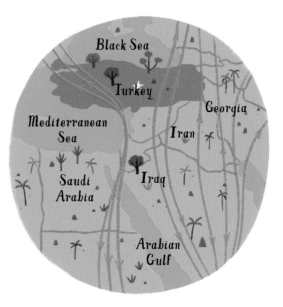

Common crane
(Grus grus)
Common cranes are long-distance fliers. They breed in the Arctic and spend every winter in Africa.

Pallid harrier
(Circus macrourus)
During migration, these harriers fly up high, where the stronger winds help them travel faster.

Bearded vulture
(Gypaetus barbatus)
These huge birds break open bones to reach the rich marrow inside.

Black vulture
(Aegypius monachus)
Although black vultures are often seen among migrating birds, they are residents in the region.

Short-toed snake eagle
(Circaetus gallicus)
These fairly large eagles
catch snakes in their
long talons.

Black stork (Ciconia nigra)
Satellite tracking has discovered
that black storks fly 7,000 km
(4,300 mi) in around 80 days
during migration.

Imperial eagle *(Aquila heliaca)*
Gliding on hot air currents and
the wind, imperial eagles can
fly at 80 km/h (50 mph).

Black kite *(Milvus migrans)*
The black kites' name is
confusing because these
birds are actually brown
with black wing tips.

Booted eagle
(Hieraaetus pennatus)
Booted eagles have
feathers all the way down
to their talons.

White pelican
*(Pelecanus
onocrotalus)*
White pelicans breed
in the swamp lands
of the Danube Delta,
Romania. In winter,
they travel down to
southern Africa.

ARABIAN DESERT

The wild Arabian Desert has very low biodiversity. It is Asia's largest desert and receives very little rainfall. The sandy landscape includes red dunes, rocks, and areas of deadly quicksand. Few animals can survive in an environment where temperatures reach 50°C (122°F) and plants struggle to grow. Vegetation is essential to most animals, even meat-eaters, because they hunt the animals that graze on foliage.

Eurasian hoopoe (*Upupa epops*)
Hoopoes raise their dramatic crests when they are excited or if another hoopoe trespasses on their territory.

Arabian gazelle (*Gazella arabica*)
Elegant gazelles live in undisturbed rocky landscapes, where they are safe from poachers.

Caracal (*Caracal caracal*)
This lynx is the only cat that can catch flying birds in midair.

Camel spider (*Galeodes arabs*)
Camel spiders are very aggressive. When they encounter humans, they are more likely to bite than run away!

Greater Egyptian jerboa (*Jaculus orientalis*)
Jerboas do not walk like mice, they hop like kangaroos.

There are some places in the desert with water but usually it does not come as rain. Instead, underground springs form pools and create oases where plants grow and animals thrive. Part of the desert is known as the Empty Quarter, or Rub' al-Khali, because it contains almost no life. Strong winds blow the sand into 250 m (820 ft) dunes that constantly change shape and position, making it difficult for plants to take root. Many insects survive the arid climate and locust swarms were once common.

Saudi Arabia

UAE

Red Sea

Yemen

Oman

Arabian Sea

Dromedary camel (*Camelus dromedarius*)
These camels are domesticated and no longer live wild. They are thought to have been first tamed on the Arabian Peninsula.

Egg-eating snake (*Dasypeltis scabra*)
For protection, the harmless egg-eating snake has evolved to look like the venomous saw-scaled viper (*Echis carinatus*).

Arabian bustard (*Ardeotis arabs*)
There may be as few as 50 bustards left in the Arabian desert.

Spiny tailed lizard (*Uromastyx aegyptia*)
The muscular spiky tail is used as a weapon to strike predators.

GREAT INDIAN PLAINS

The Great Plains cover northern India, Pakistan, Bangladesh, and part of Nepal. The whole area is a flood plain, a landscape dominated by the Ganges River. Every spring, melting snow from the Himalayas brings huge qualities of floodwater downstream. This brings in rich mud, perfect for growing plants that support farmers and wildlife.

It is the world's most intensively farmed land and home to hundreds of millions of people. This means that more of the natural habitats are being lost. Birds and small mammals can sometimes adapt and learn to live alongside people, but most big mammals are increasingly threatened. Some, like rhinos, are even changing their habits by coming out at night instead of during the day. The rarest species now live only inside the protection of national parks.

Sloth bear (*Melursus ursinus*)
Ants are the most important part of this bears' diet. They suck them up with a loud slurping sound.

Indian rhinoceros
(*Rhinoceros unicornis*)
Folklore experts believe that this single-horned rhino is one possible origin for the story of the unicorn found in mythology.

Indian roller (*Coracias benghalensis*)
Rollers earn their name during the nesting season when they perform displays of twisting, diving, soaring, and rolling through the air.

Blackbuck
(*Antilope cervicapra*)
Blackbucks have horns that grow throughout their lives and never drop off as antlers do.

King cobra
(Ophiophagus hannah)

A hissing cobra that rears up and shows its fangs is not angry—it is frightened! The shy cobra is simply telling other animals to keep away.

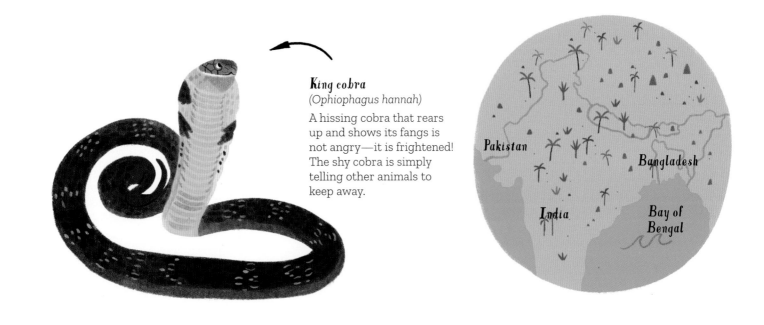

Pakistan

Bangladesh

India

Bay of Bengal

Brown fishing owl
(Ketupa zeylonensis)

Fishing owls have waterproof feathers that stop them from becoming waterlogged when they snatch a fish from the river.

Gharial
(Gavialis gangeticus)

Gharials are fish eaters. They swallow their prey whole and cannot chew.

Indian peafowl *(Pavo cristatus)*

Female peafowl are called peahens and only males are peacocks.

Whistling dog/dhole
(Cuon alpinus)

This endangered species lives in large packs and hunts during the day.

ASIAN ELEPHANT

The elephant is the national animal of Thailand, which is home to approximately 4,000 elephants. Around half of these are domesticated and the others live wild in reserves. Elephants are Asia's largest land animal, weighing up to 5 tonnes (5.5 tons), which is much less than African elephants. Their huge bodies need lots of food, so elephants spend about 16 hours every day eating. They feed on grass, leaves, and tree bark. Elephants are often found close to water; they need to drink often because their food is very dry.

Most female elephants do not have tusks and only some males grow them. Tusks are used for digging up roots or taking bark from trees. Elephants are right-tusked or left-tusked—as people are right- or left-handed. The tusk they use most is always the shortest because it wears down more quickly. Wild elephants live up to 60 years and are one of the longest-lived mammals.

Flappy ears
Asian elephants have much smaller ears than their African cousins. They flap them to fan themselves in the heat.

Splash time!
Elephants love playing in water. They roll over, suck in water with their trunks, and spray it over their entire body.

Muscular trunk
An elephant's trunk has 50,000 muscles. There are only 600 muscles in the entire human body.

Hairy babies
Young elephants have lots of hair. This rubs away as they get older.

Long-distance swimmers
Elephants are excellent swimmers. They use their trunks as snorkels and can travel very long distances in the water.

84

HUMAN USES FOR ELEPHANTS

Thailand

Putting on a show
Elephants are painted and covered with elaborate cloths for special ceremonies such as weddings.

Tasty treats
Hungry elephants will sometimes stand on their back legs to reach tasty food.

Beasts of burden
Humans have been using elephants to carry heavy loads for around 4,000 years.

National symbols
A symbol of good fortune, the elephant appeared on a former flag of Thailand.

Tourist attractions
Elephant parks are a controversial tourist attraction where animal welfare is not always the first priority.

85

Rhinoceros hornbill
(Buceros rhinoceros)

Rhinoceros hornbills can find fruit to eat all year round in a tropical rain forest.

Proboscis monkey
(Nasalis larvatus)

These monkeys are potbellied! This is because they eat hard-to-digest leaves that stay in their stomachs for a long time.

Orangutan *(Pongo pygmaeus)*

Orangutans are critically endangered apes that live only in two places—Sumatra and Borneo.

Giant thorny stick insect
(Trachyaretaon brueckneri)

Females are twice the size of males. They look dangerous but eat only leaves.

BORNEO LOWLAND RAIN FOREST

Animal life thrives in a rain forest. Year-round warmth means a ready supply of food and it is never too cold for basic survival. But the rain forest is also an extremely dangerous habitat. Animals on grassland are able to spot potential predators easily. But in rain forests animals also have to know what is going on in the trees above and below them. In the hot, tangled forest, vines twine around the broadleaf trees and wild pigs, oxen, rhinos, and elephants walk beneath. Monkeys and gibbons, mostly endangered, move through the branches. Insects swarm and snakes and lizards hunt. Most dramatic are our largest tree-dwelling animals, the gingery-red orangutans. There are around 55,000 of these left in the wild. They have long arms and both their hands and feet are excellent at gripping branches. There is much to learn about life in the treetops and babies stay with their mothers for seven years.

South China Sea

Celebes Sea

Borneo

Java Sea

Red-headed krait
(*Bungarus flaviceps*)
Highly venomous, kraits use their bite to catch prey.

Abah River flying frog
(*Rhacophorus nigropalmatus*)
Flying frogs have long toes connected by webs of skin that help them glide between trees.

Giant millipede
(*Archispirostreptus gigas*)
The word "millipede" means 1,000 legs but most have only around 400.

Binturong
(*Arctictis binturong*)
Binturongs have prehensile tails that can hold on to branches like a fifth limb.

Tree nymph
(*Idea stolli*)
The butterflies' unmistakable wing patterns and shades warn predators that they do not taste good.

EUROPE

Europe has it's own central heating system! This is the nickname given to the Gulf Stream. This sea current helps keep Europe warmer and wetter than places at similar latitude. Although some of its landscape lies inside the Arctic, most of Europe doesn't experience extreme high or low temperatures. There is enough rainfall to sustain healthy temperate forests and grasslands without producing the widespread flooding found in the tropics. There are also valuable mountain habitats in the Alps and Pyrenees, plus globally important wetlands such as the Danube Delta, that attract hundreds of species that rely on water and mud.

1 BRITAIN and IRELAND

Atlantic Oakwoods of Borrowdale, Lake District, England.

The misty fellsides of Borrowdale are rich in mysterious oakwoods. Part of an ancient forest, this is a place to glimpse the striped faces of badgers or a blur of red as squirrels quarrel above.

2 SCANDINAVIA

The snowy winters of Scandinavia provide the backdrop to a cast of iconic Arctic wildlife; reindeer and their herders live alongside moose, owls, and wild swans.

4 SPAIN and PORTUGAL

The oaks grow bark from which we make cork. The forests provide an ideal hunting ground for predators like the Iberian lynx and much, much more.

3 FRANCE, BELGIUM and the NETHERLANDS

Folklore surrounds the stork. They bring luck to the north and sometimes, it is said, babies!

Mosquito
(*Aedes nigripes*)

Arctic char
(*Salvelinus alpinus*)

Great gray (grey) owl
(*Strix nebulosa*)

Brown bear
(*Ursus arctos*)

Chamois
(*Rupicapra rupicapra*)

Moose
(*Alces alces*)

Bearded vulture
(*Gypaetus barbatus*)

Wolverine
(*Gulo gulo*)

Badger
(*Meles meles*)

Red squirrel
(*Sciurus vulgaris*)

Great spotted woodpecker
(*Dendrocopos major*)

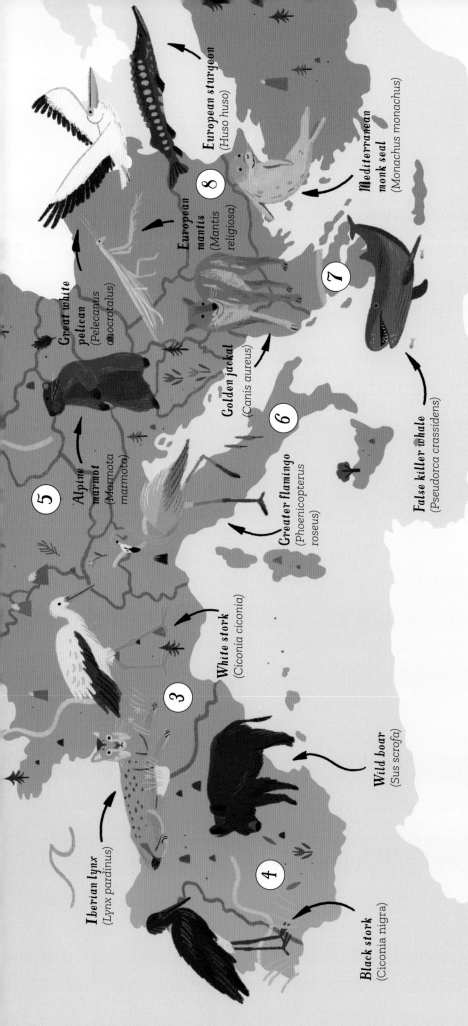

Iberian lynx
(Lynx pardinus)

Black stork
(Ciconia nigra)

Wild boar
(Sus scrofa)

White stork
(Ciconia ciconia)

Great white pelican
(Pelecanus onocrotalus)

Alpine marmot
(Marmota marmota)

Golden jackal
(Canis aureus)

Greater flamingo
(Phoenicopterus roseus)

European sturgeon
(Huso huso)

European mantis
(Mantis religiosa)

Mediterranean monk seal
(Monachus monachus)

False killer whale
(Pseudorca crassidens)

The water of the Mediterranean Sea is never cold, even in winter, and provides an important habitat for many marine and coastal species.

Much of Europe's land is commercially farmed, but agriculture can be useful to animals if we choose to manage it with wildlife in mind. Scandinavian conifer forests and Portugal's cork woodlands are grown for human use, but they make superb habitats for many other species.

Top predators, like bears and wolves, have almost disappeared from western Europe but are doing well farther east. Both species can still be found in the wild areas of Romania and Bulgaria.

(5) GERMANY, AUSTRIA, and SWITZERLAND

The word "alp" originally meant "white." The Alps have snow, rain, ice, glaciers, and avalanches. They also have warm summers and are home to super-cute marmots and agile chamois.

(7) GREECE

The mountains and islands of Greece attract all kinds of surprising wildlife, including dolphins that look like whales, beetles that "bleed" from their mouth and birds that store their dinner on thorns.

(6) ITALY
Molentargius Natural Park, Sardinia

Pink flamingos are actually white! They are excellent at line dancing and the tough skin on their legs helps them thrive in toxically salty waters.

(8) THE BALKANS
Romania

From late summer, brown bears eat almost 24/7 to build up fat reserves for their winter sleep. Females give birth at the start of hibernation and the cubs suckle on their mothers' milk to service the coldest months.

Large cuckoo chick (*Cuculus canorus*) fed by **dunnock** (*Prunella modularis*)

Female cuckoos lay their eggs in the nests of other birds. Cuckoo chicks are fed by their foster parents until they are able to feed themselves.

Oak processionary moth
(*Thaumetopoea processionea*)

These caterpillars march head-to-tail around oak trees in long lines munching leaves. They can cause damage to the trees.

Southern wood ant
(*Formica rufa*)

Wood ants' nests can be 1 m (3.3 ft) high and 2 m (6.6 ft) across. They are usually built in open clearings where the Sun can help heat up the nest.

Great spotted woodpecker
(*Dendrocopos major*)

In spring, woodpeckers mark their territories by drumming on hollow tree trunks with their powerful beaks.

Common toad (*Bufo bufo*)

Common toads need water for breeding. The rest of the time, the damp forest floor is their ideal insect-hunting ground.

Purple hairstreak butterfly
(*Neozephyrus quercus*)

Purple hairstreak butterflies spend their lives high up in the canopy and rarely come down to the ground.

Wood mouse (*Apodemus sylvaticus*)

Wood mice build complicated underground tunnels among the oaks' roots.

DECIDUOUS OAK FOREST

Sometimes called Celtic forests, atmospheric Atlantic oakwoods are found on the mild and moist western edges of Britain and Ireland. These are places of mosses, gnarled tree trunks, lichens, and golden leaves. They contain two key species, the sessile oak (*Quercus petraea*) and the common oak (*Quercus robur*). Those, together with birches, rowan, and cherry, support a huge diversity of wildlife. More than 2,300 insect species rely on these woodlands for food and shelter.

Borrowdale is home to red and roe deer, owls, and woodpeckers. Animals in an oak forest often prefer one layer of the habitat. Small birds tend to keep high in the canopy, feeding on caterpillars, while over half of the butterfly species stay close to the forest floor, taking nectar from woodland flowers. Oakwoods are remnants of the ancient forest that ran the length of the whole west coast. They receive 3.5 m (11 ft) of rainfall yearly and are temperate rain forests.

Northern Ireland

Scotland

Borrowdale, Lake District

Ireland

Wales

England

English Channel

Red squirrel (*Sciurus vulgaris*)
At the end of summer, squirrels cache acorns in the forest and return to them later in the winter when food is difficult to find.

Fallow deer (*Dama dama*)
Males are called bucks and have antlers. The female is called a doe. They were introduced to England about 1,000 years ago.

Badger (*Meles meles*)
Badgers live in family groups called clans. During the day, they sleep in underground dens called setts and come out at night searching for worms, slugs, and even fruit to eat.

SCANDINAVIA

Scandinavia is the name given to a group of countries in northern Europe that incudes Norway, Sweden, and, usually, Denmark. These counties have some of the wildest habitats in Europe and contain much of its most specular wildlife—bears, wolves, and lynx. Sweden and Norway also share a long chain of mountains called the Scandes.

Scandinavian habitats are very varied. There are flatlands in the south. Farther north lie lakes, rivers, fjords, mountains, and forests of birch, pine, and spruce. Winters are long, but the night skies can come alive with the dancing lights of the aurora borealis. Inland temperatures can drop down to -50°C (-58°F).

Many of the animals that live here were once found across all of Europe. They were driven out of their traditional range by overhunting and other human activity but survive safely in Scandinavia's quiet and unpolluted landscape.

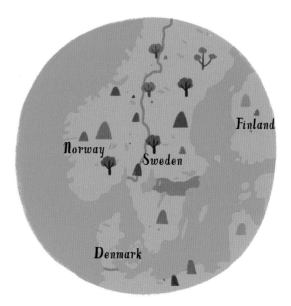

Whooper swan (*Cygnus cygnus*)
These swans pair for life. They are spring visitors to northern Scandinavia, where they raise chicks before heading south for the winter.

Wolverine (*Gulo gulo*)
Wolverines are predators famous for their strength and aggression.

Great grey (gray) owl (*Strix nebulosa*)
These owls fly so silently that they are known as ghosts of the forest.

Moor frog (*Rana arvalis*)
Brown male moor frogs turn bright blue during the breeding season.

Mosquito
(Aedes nigripes)

During the short arctic summer, there is an explosion of mosquitos.

Moose *(Alces alces)*

Moose are the world's largest deer. Only the male or bull moose have antlers.

Western capercaillie *(Tetrao urogallus)*

Capercaillies weigh up to 7 kg (15 lb) and live in Scandinavia's conifer forests. They can become very tame when living close to humans.

Arctic char
(Salvelinus alpinus)

Arctic char live much farther north than any other freshwater fish.

Northern lamprey *(Petromyzon species)*

Lampreys look like eels but are fish that live on the blood of other fish. They clamp on to a host and suck blood, which is why their other name is vampire fish.

Reindeer *(Rangifer tarandus)*

The Indigenous Sámi peoples of the far north herd semi-domesticated reindeer. Traditionally, they followed the reindeer on foot or skis.

Huge wingspans

White storks have long, wide wings, and a slow, steady flight. Wingspans of 2 m (6.5 ft) are common.

Slow growers

Young storks take a long time to grow to full size. Adults feed chicks for around nine weeks.

Showing off

Male and female storks display to each other by throwing their heads back and bill-clattering. That is, opening and snapping closed their beaks very quickly. Bill-clattering sounds a little like distant gunfire.

Unfussy eaters

White storks feed on any small animal. In water, they hunt for fish and frogs.

WHITE STORK

The striking black-and-white plumage and huge wingspan of white storks (*Ciconia ciconia*) make them impossible to miss as they migrate north. In spring, they nest on chimney caps, building giant twiggy platforms where they lay eggs and raise their young. They breed in colonies close to feeding areas, such as grassland or shallow lakes. Platforms can be used for many years and also provide homes for smaller birds, which nest within the twigs.

Nesting storks are believed to bring good luck to those living in a house. They are welcome visitors because they feed on rats and mice that are not popular roommates. At the end of summer, the storks leave to fly south to avoid the winter ice.

Myths about storks delivering babies date back at least 2,500 years. They became world famous through a short story called "The Storks" written by Danish writer Hans Christian Anderson in the nineteenth century.

Field foragers
Storks often hunt for food in fields that have just been mown or harvested. They feed on the uncovered insects and small mammals.

Migration routes
Some storks spend winter in Africa, while others stay in southern Europe.

Europe

Asia

Africa

Chimney dwellers
Storks would have once built their heavy nests high in trees. Now, they are much more likely to choose chimneys because they are more stable in stormy weather.

Genet (*Viverra genetta*)
Genets were first brought from Africa as mousers to keep homes free of rodents. The genets soon escaped and now live wild in Iberian forests

Azure-winged magpie (*Cyanopica cyanus*)
Azure-winged magpies are members of the crow family.

Red-necked nightjar (*Caprimulgus ruficollis*)
It was once believed that nightjars fed by taking milk from sleeping goats. In reality, they eat flying insects that they catch in midair.

Iberian lynx (*Lynx pardinus*)
This species has been saved from near extinction by conservation efforts.

Black stork (*Ciconia nigra*)
The Iberian Peninsula is the only place in Europe where black storks live.

Scarce swallowtail (*Iphiclides feisthamelii*)
Scarce swallowtail butterflies feed around the edges of the forest where wild flowers grow.

CORK OAK FOREST

The Iberian Peninsula contains two countries—Spain and Portugal. They are home to some of Europe's rarest and most elusive animals, found in unique habitats such as the cork forests. Cork is the soft, spongy bark of the evergreen cork oak (*Quercus suber*), a species native to the southern parts of the peninsula. Trees are not cut down to provide cork. Instead, pieces of bark are peeled off by hand. The remaining bark then starts to regrow. Each tree is harvested just once every nine years.

Much of the forest is untouched for long periods, and offers a rich, quiet habitat for wildlife. The lack of disturbance is particularly important for large, shy animals that prefer to keep away from people. In other areas, they might be hunted or simply driven away by the sight, sounds, and smell of humans. Cork is used to stopper wine bottles, for flooring, and to make cricket balls.

Bay of Biscay

Spain

Portugal

Mediterranean Sea

Stripeless tree frog
(*Hyla meridionalis*)
Frogs have smooth, damp skin; a toad's skin is rough and dry. They also move in very different ways; toads crawl slowly and frogs leap dramatically.

Death's-head hawkmoth
(*Acherontia atropos*)
The death's-head hawkmoth is named for the skull-shaped markings on its back.

Wild boar (*Sus scrofa*)
These wild pigs have no predators in the cork forests, so their population is growing.

Hedgehog (*Erinaceus europaeus*)
Hedgehogs feed on slugs, worms, and insects.

ALPS

The Alps are Europe's tallest mountains, and the range is 1,200 km (750 mi) long. Looking at the Alps during a winter storm, it seems impossible that wildlife could survive on these jagged peaks. In fact, more than 30,000 animal species live in the mountains, making them an enormously vibrant habitat. Even in midwinter there is life—tiny snow flies constantly search for food on top of the thick ice. Their bodies contain special chemicals that stop them from freezing in the sub-zero temperatures.

Bearded vulture (*Gypaetus barbatus*)
Captive-bred bearded vultures have been released in the Alps.

Alpine chough
(*Pyrrhocorax graculus*)
It is believed that Alpine choughs nest at a higher altitude than any other bird.

Apollo butterfly
(*Parnassius apollo*)
Also known as mountain butterflies, these insects are usually found at elevations of more than 1,000 m (3,300 ft).

Alpine salamander
(*Salamandra atra*)
Salamanders are difficult to spot among the rocks.

South-facing slopes are the first to start to buzz and hum in spring. They face the Sun and thaw quickly. Hibernating animals wake as the temperature rises. After six months' sleeping, they immediately start to eat. In just a few weeks, butterflies and birds appear high in the mountains, flowers and grasses grow again, and the alpine meadows fill with insects. Life has returned to the mountains.

Germany

France

Austria

Switzerland   Italy

Chamois
(Rupicapra rupicapra)
Expert mountaineers, chamois can climb almost vertical cliffs and jump up to 6 m (20 ft) between rocks.

Alpine marmot
(Marmota marmota)
During hibernation, marmots breathe just twice a minute and their heart rate slows to just five beats per minute.

Spotted nutcracker
(Nucifraga caryocatactes)
The end of a nutcracker's tongue is split in two. This helps them feel around inside pinecones to reach seeds.

Rising from the ashes

Some experts believe that legends of the phoenix—a bird that is reborn out of flames—come from the lifecycle of flamingos.

Sociable birds

Flamingos are never alone. They nest, feed, and fly in colonies or flocks.

Filter feeders

Flamingos have very fine filters around the edge of their beak that catch small water creatures.

Flamingos use mud to build cone shaped nests. These are soon dried hard by the Sun.

GREATER FLAMINGO

The Molentargius lakes in Sardinia are the perfect place to watch *genti arrubia*, or "pink people"— the Sardinian name for greater flamingos. These tall, elegant pink flamingos are, in fact, not pink at all! Their feathers are white. They bring a new meaning to the idea that "you are what you eat"! Their main food is pink shrimp (*Artemia salina*), which contain a chemical that makes them look pink. The flamingos eat thousands of shrimps and absorb the chemical, then their new feathers become pink. If the shrimp supply diminishes, the flamingos' new feathers become white again.

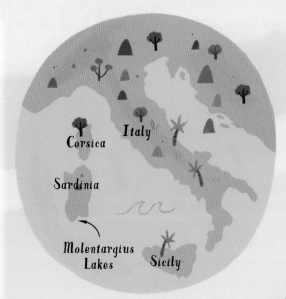

Putting on a show
Flamingos display to each other by stretching their necks up and down, then marching together in straight lines.

Changing plumage
Young flamingos start out with silvery, downy plumage that becomes white over time. Feathers don't turn pink until they have eaten enough pink shrimps.

Topsy-turvy diners
Flamingos feed with their heads upside down in the water.

Molentragius lakes are one of the most important sites in Europe for water birds. They are home to ducks, waders, and herons and by midsummer there can be more than 1,000 adult flamingos and chicks feeding in the unpolluted water. The adult flamingos recognize their chicks by the sound of their voices.

GREECE

Greece is a country of mountains and islands. Much of its wildlife is shy and difficult to find in the rocky landscape, while others can be easily seen in hotel gardens.

Greece has around 6,000 islands and an extremely long coastline. Some of the country's most interesting animals live in the sea and can only be spotted on boat trips. Currently, the National Marine Park of Alonissos is the largest protected marine reserve in Europe. It was first established to provide a safe habitat for endangered monk seals, but now shelters a range of whales, dolphins, and more than 300 species of fish.

Greece has 12 other national parks, such as Mount Oeta, where the legendary hero Hercules is supposed to have died. Today, the parks protect rich forests and many of the country's rarest animals. They also supply food for migrating birds on the route between northern Europe and Africa.

Great grey (gray) shrike
(Lanius excubitor)
Known as butcher birds, these hunters store prey on sharp thorns to eat later.

European nightjar *(Caprimulgus europaeus)*
European nightjars are camouflaged to match forest habitats.

Etruscan shrew *(Suncus etruscus)*
Etruscan shrews are the world's smallest mammals. They are active animals that need to eat twice their own bodyweight every day.

Bloody-nosed beetle *(Timarcha tenebricosa)*
As their name suggests, when facing an enemy, these beetles release a drop of bright red liquid from their mouth. This tastes terrible and predators learn to keep away.

European mantis
(Mantis religiosa)
Females are much larger than males. After mating, the female will sometimes eat the male!

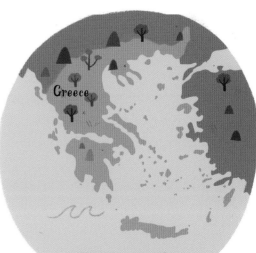

Greece

Mediterranean Sea

Hummingbird hawkmoth
(Macroglossum stellatarum)

Hawkmoths look like hummingbirds. They have a 58 mm (2 in) wingspan and hover above flowers to feed.

Golden jackal
(Canis aureus)

Similar to but much smaller than wolves, jackals eat small mammals and insects.

Mediterranean monk seal
(Monachus monachus)

A critically endangered species, there may be as few as 600 of these seals remaining.

Jersey tiger
(Euplagia quadripunctaria)

In late May on the island of Rhodes, millions of Jersey tiger moths rest in shady valleys.

False killer whale *(Pseudorca crassidens)*

These dolphins were once thought to be closely related to orca—killer whales. But their diet is very different—false killers feed mainly on fish and squid.

BROWN BEAR

Brown bears (*Ursus arctos*) once roamed over almost all of Europe. They are intelligent, highly adaptable, and, because of their size and strength, have no natural predators—other than people. Over centuries, humans hunted bears or took over their best habitats. As a result, bears disappeared in many countries—but not Romania. More than half of all Europe's brown bears live in Romania's ancient forests.

Romania

Peril on the roads
Road traffic is a major danger for all wildlife, even large animals like bears.

Scavengers
Some Romanian brown bears have learned to visit cities at night. They upend and search through wastebags, looking for an easy meal.

An adult bear weighs 450 kg (1,000 lb) and has a very healthy appetite! They can spend 18 hours a day searching for food. Bears are true omnivores—they are not fast enough to catch live prey but they will eat any carrion they find in the forest. However, most of their diet is made up of plants, and in late summer they eat fruit, mushrooms, and nuts.

Brown bears are careful to avoid humans. Attacks are very rare and usually only happen when bears are surprised or frightened.

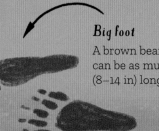

Big foot
A brown bear's hind paws can be as much as 21–36 cm (8–14 in) long.

Underground sleepers
During winter, brown bears hibernate in caves, under tree roots, or in dens dug into the earth.

Scanning the horizon
Bears are shortsighted and will stand up on their back legs to get a better view of their surroundings.

Fishy feast
Bears eat fish—when they can catch them!

Grassy grazers
Grass and insects provide a large part of a bear's diet.

Staying close to mother
Bear cubs will stay with their mother until they are around three years old.

Mad about apples
Apples are one of the bears' best-loved foods.

DANUBE DELTA HABITAT

The River Danube begins in Germany's Black Forest region. It flows through ten countries—more than any other river—and finally empties into the Black Sea.

Just before the river reaches the sea, it becomes slower and widens out over a huge area. This is called a delta and it creates a complicated maze of water channels, swamps, and pools.

The Danube Delta is on the border between Ukraine and Romania, and covers 4,150 sq km (1,600 sq mi). It is a wonderfully biodiverse habitat of international importance. For instance, more than 300 bird species have been spotted, and scientists are still trying to count the number of insect species that are found there.

Although people live in the delta, this wetland landscape is one of the least populated places in Europe. This is a region of lakes, reeds, marshes, and forests, much of it difficult to reach. Wildlife is largely undisturbed, though tourism is raising concerns in some areas.

Water buffalo (*Bubalus bubalis*)
Water buffalo have been released into the delta to graze on water plants, so stopping the channels from becoming blocked.

Marsh frog (*Pelophylax ridibundus*)
These clever frogs often hitch a ride on the back of water buffalos so they can picnic on the insects the buffalos attract.

Emperor dragonfly (*Anax imperator*)
Dragonflies are fast, powerful predators. They hunt butterflies, other dragonflies, and even take tadpoles out of the water!

Raccoon dog (*Nyctereutes procyonoides*)
These members of the dog family were introduced to Europe from Asia as a result of the fur trade. They are an invasive species of concern.

European bee-eater
(*Merops apiaster*)

To nest, bee-eaters excavate tunnels in sandy riverbanks.

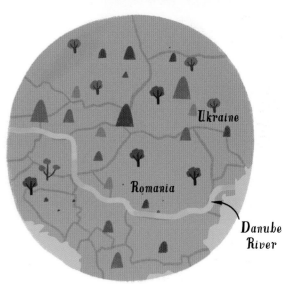

Ukraine

Romania

Danube River

European sturgeon (*Huso huso*)

The unfertilized eggs of the sturgeon are called roe. They are eaten as caviar.

Great white pelican
(*Pelecanus onocrotalus*)

More than half of Europe's great white pelicans breed in the Danube Delta.

Wels catfish
(*Silurus glanis*)

These catfish can live for 50 years and reach an impressive 3 m (10 ft) long.

Pond turtle
(*Emys orbicularis*)

Pond turtles lay their eggs on land.

Water shrew (*Neomys fodiens*)

Tiny water shrews pack a punch—or rather a bite! They are one of the few mammals that have a venomous bite.

OCEANIA

Oceania is home to more domestic sheep than people! It lies largely within the southern hemisphere and so has winter in June, July, and August, while summer begins in December! Oceania is not a continent as such but a geographical area that covers all of the Pacific nations, apart from those that are included in Asia. Countries on other continents are connected by land, but those in Oceania are linked by sea. The islands are in isolated groups scattered around a vast ocean, each with its own diverse and exciting collection of wildlife.

Polar bear
(*Ursus maritimus*)

Musk ox
(*Ovibos moschatus*)

Narwhal
(*Monodon monoceros*)

Walrus
(*Odobenus rosmarus*)

Coconut crab
(*Birgus latro*)

Giant Pacific octopus
(*Enteroctopus dofleini*)

Snowy owl
(*Bubo scandiacus*)

(4) THE ARCTIC
The Arctic is home to the polar bear, to the musk oxen that defend their young by forming protective circles around them, and to the narwhals that have a very cool connection to the mythical unicorn!

(2) NEW ZEALAND
New Zealand's wildlife is great at springing surprises—there are ultra-smart birds that have lost the ability to fly and at least one type of insect with ears on its legs!

(1) AUSTRALIA
Australia is a land of wonderfully unlikely animals—fierce Tasmanian devils, the unbelievable duck-billed platypus, and the super-cute bilby, just for starters.

Australia is the smallest of the world's continents, but it is the biggest landmass in Oceania. The central regions are dry and hot, a suitable habitat for only the most specialized wildlife. Australia is famous for its extraordinary marsupials—pouched animals.

Most of Oceania is warm and wet. But the Pacific extends into both the north and south polar regions. Life in these extreme environments requires completely different adaptations that enable the animals that live there to survive the long, dark winters.

Oceania is threatened by climate change. Any rise in global temperature melts more of the polar ice and raises the world's sea levels. Most of the land on the remote Marshall Islands is just 2.1 m (6.9 ft) above the sea. If the Pacific Ocean water level grows higher, the islands will almost certainly be flooded.

Flying fish
(*Cheilopogon pinnatibarbatus*)

Kiwi
(*Apteryx australis*)

Giant weta
(*Deinacrida rugosa*)

Koala
(*Phascolarctos cinereus*)

Kakapo
(*Strigops habroptilus*)

Lumholtz's tree kangaroo
(*Dendrolagus lumholtzi*)

Duck-billed platypus
(*Ornithorhynchus anatinus*)

Short-beaked echidna
(*Tachyglossus aculeatus*)

3 PACIFIC OCEAN
The Pacific contains so much life and variety. There are smiley spiders, flying fish, and puzzle-solving octopuses!

5 THE ANTARCTIC
Try to imagine the most hostile environment for any bird to live and breed in—permanent ice, near 24-hour darkness, gale-force winds, and little shelter. This is the Antarctic and ingenious emperor penguins have learned to survive here against all odds.

Emperor penguin
(*Aptenodytes forsteri*)

Orca
(*Orcinus orca*)

AUSTRALIA

Australia was cut off from all other continents around 45 million years ago. After the dinosaurs became extinct, a whole range of new animals evolved, including a group called marsupials. Eventually, marsupials almost completely disappeared from most places—apart from Australia, where they make up almost all of the mammal species.

Marsupial means "pouch." Pouches are small pockets of skin next to the females' stomach. They keep young marsupials warm, dry, and protected. Marsupial mothers give birth to very small babies that cannot survive by themselves. They spend the first few weeks inside the pouch, feeding on their mother's milk and growing very quickly. As they get bigger, the young leave the pouch to explore but dart back inside to sleep or to hide from anything dangerous.

Red kangaroos are the biggest marsupials. Adults weigh up to 46 kg (101.4 lb) but their babies weigh just 1 g (0.03 oz) and are 2 cm (0.8 in) long.

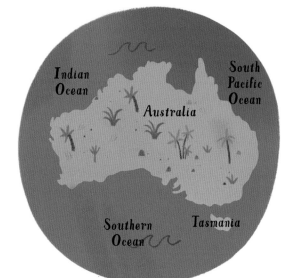

Bilby (*Macrotis lagotis*)
Female bilbies are pregnant for just 14 days before giving birth to their tiny babies.

Sugar glider (*Petaurus breviceps*)
Sugar gliders use flaps of skin between their legs to glide between trees at night.

Red kangaroo (*Osphranter rufus*)
These are the largest kangaroos. They are active mostly at night and can be difficult to see on the highway. Young kangaroos are called joeys, females are known as fliers, and males are called boomers.

Tasmanian devil
(*Sarcophilus harrisii*)
Tasmanian devils are only found on the island of Tasmania. They are efficient hunters but prefer to eat carrion when possible.

Lumholtz's tree kangaroo
(Dendrolagus lumholtzi)

As their name suggests, tree- kangaroos live in the trees, feeding on leaves and fruit. They have long, sharp claws and strong back legs for climbing.

Duck-billed platypus
(Ornithorhynchus anatinus)

Is it a bird? Or is it a rodent? The duck-billed platypus is truly strange. It is a mammal that lays eggs instead of giving birth to live young.

Western quoll *(Dasyurus geoffroii)*

Quolls are the largest native carnivore on mainland Australia. They are about the size of domestic cats.

Striped possum or common striped possum
(Dactylopsila trivirgata)

These possums live in the rain forests in northeast Australia. They give off a very strong smell that is thought to drive away predators.

Southern hairy-nosed wombat
(Lasiorhinus latifrons)

Wombats are expert burrowers. They dig long tunnels and dens that are shared with up to ten other wombats.

Koala
(Phascolarctos cinereus)

Koalas live in eucalyptus trees and only eat eucalyptus leaves. They sleep for up to 20 hours each day.

FOREST HABITAT

The first humans reached New Zealand approximately 800 years ago. They found a group of islands covered with vast forests of southern beech and rimu trees and teeming with animals. The forests provide shelter and food for many diverse plants and animals. Before the arrival of people, the only native land mammals on the islands were three species of bat. There were no large predators.

Morepork owl *(Ninox novaeseelandiae)*

These owls are known for their haunting two-tone call that sounds just like "more-pork, more-pork."

Kakapo *(Strigops habroptilus)*

Kakapos are the world's only flightless parrots. They probably live longer than any other bird—up to 100 years.

New Zealand fantail *(Rhipidura fuliginosa)*

When dainty fantails display, their tail feathers stand upright and open up like a giant fan.

Yellow-eyed penguin *(Megadyptes antipodes)*

Most penguins like to nest close to each other, but yellow-eyed penguins prefer to be completely out of sight of the rest of the colony.

Giant weta *(Deinacrida rugosa)*

A giant weta's ears are on its front legs, just under the knee joint.

As a result, many of New Zealand's birds lost the power of flight. That was not a problem until the introduction by humans of predators like weasels and rats. The flightless birds were easy prey and their populations dwindled. From ground-dwelling invertebrates, lizards, and frogs to canopy-living birds, the temperate forests play host to complex life webs. Surprisingly, New Zealand is the best place to see penguins—it is home to 13 of the world's 18 species, at least one of which nests inside the forest.

Tasman Sea

New Zealand

South Pacific Ocean

New Zealand wood pigeon or **kererū**
(Hemiphaga novaeseelandiae)
These birds are fruit-eaters. Their population has been decimated by the introduction of brush-tailed possums *(Trichosurus vulpecula)*.

Kiwi *(Apteryx australis)*
Kiwis are the only birds that have nostrils at the very end of their beaks.

Lesser short-tailed bat
(Mystacina tuberculata)
Short-tailed bats find a lot of their food by crawling around the forest floor looking for insects among the fallen leaves.

Tuatara *(Sphenodon punctatus)*
Young tuataras have three eyes. The extra one is in the middle of their forehead and becomes covered in scales by the time the lizard is six months old.

Jewelled gecko
(Naultinus gemmeus)
Female geckos are much brighter than the brown males.

PACIFIC OCEAN

The Pacific is the world's largest ocean. It covers nearly one third of the Earth's surface. There are more than 25,000 islands scattered throughout this vast area. Most of the islands are tropical, offering a rich, warm environment but surprisingly few animal species. This is because of the remoteness of the habitats that are isolated from other islands. While seabirds and marine life have no difficulty moving around the ocean, smaller animals must stay in one place. Land mammals are rare. However, many islands have healthy populations of invertebrates. These were probably carried in by the wind or on floating logs.

The greatest biodiversity of the Pacific Ocean is found in the sea. For example, Hawaii, one of the main island groups, is approximately 3,000 km (1,860 mi) from any large landmass. It has over 300 species of birds but most are seabirds that spend 80 percent of their lives feeding in the open ocean.

Flying fish
(Cheilopogon pinnatibarbatus)
Flying fish leap out of the water to avoid predators. They can travel in the air for up to 50 m (160 ft). They glide using long fins on each side of their body.

Frilled shark
(Chlamydoselachus anguineus)
Frilled sharks have 300 sharp, curved teeth.

Coconut crab
(Birgus latro)
Coconut crabs can grow up to 1 m (3 ft 3 in) and weigh 4 kg (9 lb). They live in underground burrows but often climb trees to reach nuts and fruit to eat.

Giant Pacific octopus
(Enteroctopus dofleini)
Octopuses are super-intelligent predators that feed on small sea creatures. They catch their prey using powerful suckers and eat with a sharp beak hidden between their tentacles.

Happy-face spider
(Theridion grallator)

Smiley, happy-face spiders live on the Hawaiian Islands. Their name comes from markings on their abdomen that look like a smiling face.

Hawaiian honeycreeper
(Drepanis coccinea)

The long, thin, curved beaks of these bright birds have evolved to drink nectar from deep inside flowers.

Whitemargin stargazer
(Uranoscopus sulphureus)

These fish hide in sand on the seabed with just their eyes and mouth showing. They lie in wait until a small fish gets near, then they spring out to grab it.

Southern cassowary
(Casuarius casuarius)

Cassowaries stand 1.8 m (6 ft) tall and have an extremely powerful kick.

Thorny devil *(Moloch horridus)*

Thorny devils are covered with sharp spines. When predators approach, they put their head between their legs and the enemy is faced with a barrage of spines.

Giant golden-crowned flying fox
(Acerodon jubatus)

These come from the Philippines and are part of the family called megabats.

Short-beaked echidna
(Tachyglossus aculeatus)

The echidna's long spines are home to the world's biggest fleas.

THE ARCTIC

The Arctic is not a single place. It covers the northern regions of seven different countries and is a zone of extremes. The North Pole lies in a sea that is frozen all year. At the start of winter, most of the Arctic Ocean also freezes. Marine mammals, such as whales, need to find the edge of the ice so that can feed and breathe.
In summer, half of the winter sea ice melts and the ocean opens up again.

Most wildlife lives farther south on land, close to the Arctic Circle. Unlike the isolated Antarctic, animals can easily reach the Arctic and that produces an environment with a much higher biodiversity. Wildlife has to survive punishing weather conditions and constantly changing day lengths. In the polar winter, the Sun never rises above the horizon, so it is dark for 24 hours a day. The exact opposite, midnight Sun, occurs in summer—when it never goes dark.

Snowy owl *(Bubo scandiacus)*
Snowy owls are the only white species of owl. This helps camouflage the birds as they hunt in a snowy landscape.

Beluga whale
(Delphinapterus leucas)
Beluga whales communicate between themselves using high-pitched squeals. whistles, and squeaks. They are often called sea canaries.

Musk ox *(Ovibos moschatus)*
Underneath their long, waterproof hair, musk ox grow thick, soft fur called qiviut. This is the world's warmest wool and is used to knit scarves and hats.

Narwhal
(Monodon monoceros)
Male narwhals have a long, twisted tusk on the top of their head. In medieval times, these were traded as unicorn horns.

Ivory gull *(Pagophila eburnea)*

Ivory gulls live in the cold waters of the North Pacific. They are Arctic specialists that are severely threatened by global warming and the melting of polar ice.

Arctic Ocean

Horned stalked jellyfish *(Lucernaria quadricornis)*

These jellyfish are predators armed with hundreds of tentacles that grab any small animal that swims within reach.

Walrus *(Odobenus rosmarus)*

Both male and female walruses have tusks. They are used as grips when walruses climb on to floating ice.

King eider *(Somateria spectabilis)*

King eiders are sea ducks that move inland on to the tundra to breed in early summer.

Fish doctor *(Gymnelus viridis)*

Fish doctors are ray-finned fish that live in the mud and sand on the seabed of the Arctic Ocean.

Polar bear *(Ursus maritimus)*

Polar bears are the world's largest land predators. They hunt seals on the frozen Arctic seas, where they are known as ice bears.

THE ANTARCTIC

The Antarctic is the coldest of all continents. Winters are harsh and very long, so most birds move farther north, where survival is easier. Emperor penguins (*Aptenodytes forsteri*) are the only species that nests in these hostile conditions.

Male and female penguins leave the sea at the start of winter. They walk up to 120 km (75 mi) to reach their breeding grounds on the Antarctic mainland. After mating, each female lays one egg and immediately walks back to the sea. Each male balances an egg on his feet and holds it against an area of warm skin called a brood patch. For the next ten weeks, the males do not eat or move. Their job is to stop the eggs from freezing in temperatures that can drop as low as −30°C (−22°F).

Female penguins usually return just after the chicks have hatched. They bring food back for the chick and take over the job of protection, allowing the hungry males to go back to sea and feed.

Sticking together
There are thousands of penguins in the breeding colony. They huddle close together to keep warm, with their backs to the wind.

High jumpers
Super-charged penguins jump out on to the ice by diving deep into the water and swimming up as fast as possible.

Taking shelter
Young penguins can easily die in the cold, so they stay beneath an adult's feathers.

Safety in numbers
Young emperor penguins huddle together for warmth while waiting for their parents to return with food.

Only child
Emperor penguins lay just one egg a year. It would be impossible for males to balance two eggs on their feet.

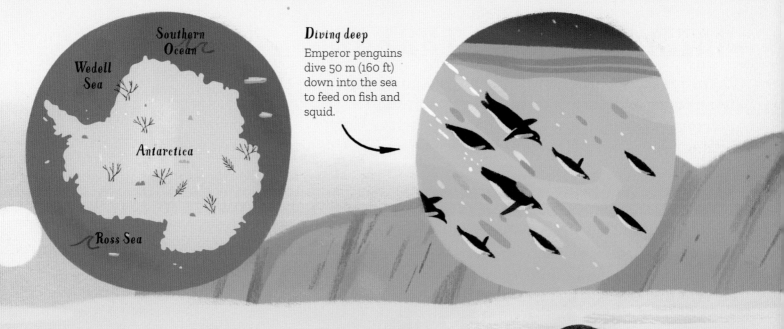

Southern Ocean

Wedell Sea

Antarctica

Ross Sea

Diving deep

Emperor penguins dive 50 m (160 ft) down into the sea to feed on fish and squid.

Shufflers

Penguins' short legs make walking slow. They often slide over the ice when they find a downward slope.

Orca (*Orcinus orca*)

Pods of hungry orca often patrol the water close to the ice, waiting for emperor penguins to set off on fishing trips.

Huge colonies

By the end of the breeding season there can be 50,000 emperor penguins in a colony.

ANIMALS UNDER THREAT

There are approximately 6,500 species of mammals living today and scientists estimate that around a quarter—1,600 species—are in danger of extinction. Extinction is a natural process. New species evolve and others vanish. However, modern human activity is accelerating change faster than ever before, so animals have no time to evolve. Overhunting and pollution endanger wildlife around the world; and habitat destruction is fatal for many species. When forests are cut down, the resident animals often have nowhere to go. Without exactly the right kind of food and shelter most species simply cannot survive.

The fur trade
Some animals are illegally hunted for fur to make coats and hats.

CLIMATE CHANGE—THE BIGGEST THREAT OF ALL

Life on Earth would be impossible without the Sun. It provides the heat and light that allows plants and animals to survive. But they all need a "habitable zone"—an environment that is not too hot and not too cold, but just right.

Humans produce excess greenhouses gases, such as carbon dioxide and methane. These gases form a layer over the atmosphere that acts like a blanket and stops heat escaping. The planet is becoming warmer. Rising temperatures melt the polar ice, change the weather, and alter most of the world's habitats—threatening the survival of all life.

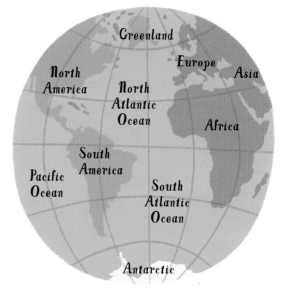

Pollution from vehicles
Buildings and roads now stand where once there were trees and grassland. Vehicles emit gases that contribute to climate change and damage health.

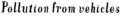

Deforestation

Every 6 seconds, an area of rain forest the size of a football pitch is cut down.

Endangered birds

Only around 500 northern bald ibis are left in the wild. Hunting and pesticides have brought them close to extinction.

Habitat loss

Orang-utans are critically endangered because of poaching and deforestation.

The pet trade

Tortoises and other small animals are still taken from the wild and sold as pets.

PEOPLE AND ANIMALS

There were animals on Earth long before the first humans appeared. The whole history of our species is closely connected to wildlife. At first, our ancestors hunted animals for food and skins, then they learned how to farm some species for meat, eggs, and milk. Slowly, over thousands of years, we changed some species. Wolves evolved into dogs and the red junglefowl became farmyard chickens.

But along the way humans were careless, and overhunting wiped out entire species like the dodo and passenger pigeon. As animals started to disappear, conservationists realized that we needed to take care of all wildlife before it was too late.

Giant salamander studies
Scientists study rare species like giant salamanders to understand the best way to help them survive.

TAKING CARE

In 1783, the Bogd Khan Uul Reserve in Mongolia became the very first national park. Since then, parks have been created all over the world, protecting habitats and wildlife. The biggest is the Northeast Greenland National Park, a tundra landscape larger than most countries.

A protected habitat
More than 10,000 musk-ox live in the vast Northeast Greenland National Park, where they are legally protected.

Attracting animals
People have discovered the pleasure of feeding creatures such as this monarch butterfly in their own gardens.

WELL-BEING

Scientists have proven that humans really need contact with nature. Just walking through a forest or watching a flock of birds flying overhead reduces our stress and anxiety. Spending time with animals and plants makes us feel happier and more relaxed. Humans are not separate from the natural world—we are part of it.

Breeding plan

Conservationists help rare species like Andean condors by breeding them in captivity and releasing the youngsters into the wild.

Domesticating wolves

Thousands of years ago, humans took wolf cubs from the wild and over time, they evolved into the dogs we know today.

Friendly faces

In places like the Galápagos, where all hunting has been banned, many of the islands' animals have completely lost their fear of humans.

Protective reserves

The Bogd Khan Uul Reserve in Mongolia was created to prevent animals like wild boar being wiped out by overhunting.

ECOTOURISM

A whole new type of travel has recently opened up, called ecotourism. It takes visitors to see exciting animals in wonderful places. Every year, millions of people head to Africa to photograph gorillas and lions. People are now hunting animals with cameras rather than guns, which is better for everyone.

Gorillas in the wild

Every day, small numbers of people hike into the Virunga Mountains in East Africa to marvel at families of wild gorillas.

HOW TO HELP ANIMALS AND THE PLANET

Animals are essential to the planet and face many threats. Habitat loss, water pollution, and climate change all pose challenges. What can we do to help?

CONNECT WITH OTHERS

Find conservation or rescue organizations working in your area and volunteer.

Use social media to share the things you care about. There are many excellent young environmental campaigners active online.

REMEMBER— NO VOICE IS TOO SMALL!

If we each take tiny steps to protect the planet, we can go far together.

LEARN, LEARN, LEARN!

The more we know about the natural world, the better we can care for it.

- Be curious! Read, watch, listen, and learn about wildlife.

- Animals have to live somewhere! Learn about their habitats.

- Learn about the different oceans and the life they contain.

- Find out about the threats we face and how to help.

- Talk about what you are learning—with family, friends, and your wider community.

CONNECT WITH NATURE EVERY DAY

- Spend time outdoors every day if you can—in every kind of weather and season.

- Look for wildlife indoors, too. Spiders and woodlice are incredible creatures.

- Feed the birds—from your balcony, near your home, or in the park.

- Learn to look at the details of things—feathers, insects, and worms are all fascinating.

- Take photographs of wildlife you encounter—and the marks made by them, such as footprints in mud or snow. Draw or write about them.

- Make a collection of "finds" from your walks. Photograph and share them with your friends.

- Keep a wildlife diary.

GET PERSPECTIVE

A magnifier and binoculars will help you see more of what is far away or very small.

REUSE, RECYCLE, AND TRY NOT TO WASTE— ANYTHING!

Changes in the climate are dangerous for the planet. We can all play a role in helping to slow down or even stop global warming:

- Switch off lights when you leave a room.

- Try not to buy things you do not need.

- Park the car! If you can walk or cycle to school or to see a friend safely, do!

- Try not to leave taps running.

- Think about what you eat and try to make environmentally sustainable choices. Eat more locally produced vegetables, fruits, and beans.

- Avoid single-use plastics.

GLOSSARY

Ambush predator   A hunting animal that waits for prey to come close.

Amphibian   An animal that breeds in water but spends most of its life on land.

Antarctic   Cold area around the South Pole.

Apex predator   A predator so powerful it has no enemies.

Aquatic   Species living in water.

Arctic   Cold area around the North Pole.

Bacteria   Single-cell invertebrates too small to be seen by the human eye.

Biodiverse   The variety of species living in one area.

Canopy   The upper layer of a forest beneath the emergent trees.

Carnivore   An animal that eats meat only.

Carrion   An animal's dead body.

Cold-blooded   An animal that does not produce its own body heat.

Deciduous   A plant or tree that loses its leaves in winter.

Deforestation   The cutting down of woodlands.

Domestic   An animal that has been tamed and now lives alongside humans.

Ecotourism   Journeying in a sustainable way to watch wildlife.

Grazer   An animal that eats grass.

Habitat   An animal's natural environment.

Herbivore   An animal that eats plants only.

Hibernate   Sleeping all through the winter.

Insectivorous   An animal that eats insects.

Invertebrate   An animal without a backbone.

Joey   A young marsupial.

Marine   Concerning the sea.

Marsupial	Animal species in which the female carries her young in a pouch.
Migration	A regular journey made by animals in order to find food or a breeding area.
Nectar	A sugary liquid produced by flowers.
Nocturnal	Active during the night.
Omnivore	An animal that eats meat and plants.
Polar	The cold areas around both the North and South Poles.
Predator	An animal that hunts and eats other animals.
Prehensile	An animal's tail that can be used for holding and grasping.
Prey	An animal that is killed and eaten by another animal.
Proboscis	A feeding tube used to suck up food and water.
Rain forest	A forest that receives a very large amount of rain.
Scavenger	An animal that feeds on prey that is already dead.
Shellfish	Aquatic invertebrates that live inside a hard shell.
Spawning	Laying eggs.
Swarm	A large group of flying insects.
Talons	Sharp claws on the end of birds' toes.
Temperate zones	Areas of the Earth between the tropics and polar regions.
Tentacle	An invertebrate's long limbs, used to grab food and sometimes attack enemies.
Venom	A poisonous fluid produced by an animal that kills or paralyzes prey with a bite.
Vertebrate	An animal with a backbone.
Warm-blooded	An animal that produces its own body heat.
Wingspan	The distance from one wing tip to the other.
Zooplankton	Tiny animals that live in the ocean.

INDEX